HI, THERE!

to Daddy
love
J.

HI, THERE !

GREGORY CLARK

author of
THE BEST OF GREGORY CLARK
and
GREG'S CHOICE

McGRAW-HILL RYERSON LIMITED
Toronto   Montreal   New York   London   Sydney
Mexico   Panama   Johannesburg   Düsseldorf
Rio de Janeiro   Kuala Lumpur   New Delhi   Singapore

© **THE RYERSON PRESS, 1963**

ISBN 0-7700-6026-9

First Paperback Edition, 1968

ACKNOWLEDGMENT

THE PUBLISHER AND AUTHOR
ARE GRATEFUL TO "WEEKEND MAGAZINE"
FOR PERMISSION
TO REPRINT THESE STORIES.

3 4 5 6 7 8 9 10   JD   10 9 8 7 6 5 4 3

PRINTED AND BOUND IN CANADA

FOREWORD

This is the third collection of the "shorties" which have appeared over the past few years on the inside back page of *Weekend Magazine*. They are republished with the permission of *Weekend*. In fact, this particular selection has been made by Craig Ballantyne, editorial director of *Weekend*, a circumstance that allows me the opportunity to say that it was Craig Ballantyne who invented the size, shape and colour of the storiettes which follow.

It had never occurred to me that a story could be told in a few hundred words. In my more furious years as a reporter and feature writer on the daily press, during the nineteen twenties, thirties and forties, I had roistered in thousands upon thousands of words at a time, on coronations, wars, mine disasters, murders and the founding of monumental things like the United Nations or the Vimy Memorial.

When I was offered the inside back page of *Weekend*, I was astonished to find it would hold only a few hundred words.

"It's quite simple," said Craig Ballantyne. "Write about small things."

And what a pleasure it has been, after all the sound and the fury, to write about small things.

Many people have asked me: "Are these stories true?" What a question to ask!   G. C.

CONTENTS

Toffee

IT IS with natural reluctance that I admit that I have been a toffee addict for sixty-some years.

But it is necessary to do so to explain all that excitement and confusion at my front door yesterday, that police cruiser, those two doctors, five minutes apart, dashing up the walk with their bags.

Racial prejudice inclines me toward Scotch toffee. But it is not as sticky as English treacle toffee. Treacle toffee has that same virtue that is referred to when they say a food sticks to the ribs. Treacle toffee sticks to the teeth. Many a time I have gone to sleep at night with a good gob of treacle toffee glued to my molars. And when I woke in the morning, there it was, still. I had been enjoying it in my dreams.

My vice was discovered early in my childhood, and my parents tried every device to wean me to other candies. Chocolates? I have no use for them. One squish with your tongue against the roof of the mouth and they're gone.

Though I am naturally of a vivacious and extroverted nature, I was thought, through my childhood, to be a rather speechless and taciturn boy. This was because my mouth was locked shut on a hunk of treacle toffee.

School teachers often clouted me over the head because I apparently was a rebellious pupil, stubbornly

1

refusing to answer a question. I answered as soon as I could.

I am giving you these details so that you will appreciate what happened yesterday. Many of my neighbours have telephoned since then, and I have given them the true story. But I have no doubt that those who saw the excitement and did not telephone me will have spread the news all over that I have suffered a stroke, or broken my neck or some such rumour.

Actually, the best toffee I ever encountered in a long epicurean life, as far as toffee goes, was Belgian. In one of those wars, I helped capture a small Belgian village. And in pollacking around the ruins, as soldiers do, I found this small tin box, in what likely had been the *patisserie* of the village. It contained the most delectable toffee I have ever consumed. You could clamp a piece of that toffee in your teeth and inhale it for three-quarters of an hour. The label was burned off the box, of course. Some of my friends have since become ambassadors to Belgium, trade commissioners, and so forth. I have had them scour the whole of Belgium. They never came up with it.

Another mighty toffee I met about fifteen years ago when I was down in Tennessee and Arkansas trying to buy a good beagle. Our car got stuck in the mud, and an old Negro mammy invited us into her shanty while she sent her grandson afoot in quest of a tow truck. She served us coffee and gave us a treat of her homemade toffee made with sorghum. I tell you, if I had been a man of means, I would have established that old mammy in Manchester, England, or Doncaster, or one of the great shrines of treacle toffee, and she would have made

2

a fortune for us. I would probably be a peer of the realm, by now, like those mustard lords, biscuit lords and liver-pill lords they have over there.

But in every life some rain must fall. In my fifties, I had to surrender my teeth and adopt dentures. There are those, I know, who would say that no teeth could withstand the pull, drag and wrench of half a century of toffee chewing. But my dentist tells me this is nonsense. In my case, it was more likely chewing on pipe stems, gnawing venison rib chops and munching radishes.

The shock with which I discovered that my toffee days were over, apparently, was one of the dark moments of my life. I put the usual gob of toffee in. And I nearly smothered. You can't take BOTH dentures out at the same time. And my two were cemented together.

I just soaked it through. Thereafter, for three years, by shrewdly selecting quite small splinters of toffee, I developed a certain skill. And of course, by now, I can handle the usual-size chunk. But naturally, it enjoins a period of silence each time.

Last week, my womenfolk went on a motor trip down to the States, they having not been over the border for four months, and each of them having $25 burning holes in their purses. And I was left at home here alone with Chelsea, our Corgi dog.

My sister, who lives in the country, thought she would just give me a long-distance ring to see how I was making out.

"How are you making out?" she asked brightly, when I picked up the receiver.

"Fine," I said.

But, as I had a large gob of toffee just nicely snuggled in my molars, it came out:

"Bbmmmm!"

"What's that?" she exclaimed.

"I'll call you back later," I said.

But it came out:

"Bobgumbagbmmmmmm!"

"Greg!" cried my sister.

"Aw, for Peter's sake," I said, "I'll ring you back in about 15 minutes."

But it came out:

"Gombungbeebungbaaaahhhh!"

At which moment, Chelsea found a late autumnal bee bumping around the floor, and she burst into frantic barks, for she has a high horror of bees.

"Ggmmmmm!" I yelled at her, to keep her quiet.

"Oh, you poor, poor man!" cried my sister, and hung up.

I squashed the bee and walked around the house for a little while until the toffee had subsided enough. Then I put a call through to my sister's farm.

The line was busy.

I was debating whether to take another chunk of toffee, for there were only two pieces left on the plate, when the doorbell rang loudly, and somebody at the same time rapped violently on the same door.

I opened.

It was two policemen.

"You Mr. Clark?"

"Yes, sir."

"All O.K. here?"

"Yes, sir."

"We had an emergency call," said the constable. "Said you were ill. Possibly a stroke."

"Me?" I protested.

So I invited them in and cracked up another cake of toffee and gave them a treat. We were just nicely settled into it when again the doorbell rang.

This was the first doctor. A stranger to me.

"I had an emergency call from the country," he said. "Mr. Clark?"

"Yes, sir."

"Are you all O.K.?"

"Yes, sir."

"They said you must have suffered a stroke."

So he joined the two policemen, and we were all sitting having some toffee when the second doctor, who is my own doctor, arrived. They had got him at the hospital, and he had rushed right up. (We fish together, and a doctor doesn't like to lose a fishing companion.)

About an hour later, if you were still watching, you saw my sister arrive.

By this time the doctors and the police had left.

"Have some toffee," I suggested to my sister, when she had recovered her breath and poise.

"No, THANK you!" she said.

Pixie

AS I THREADED my way through the mid-afternoon downtown throngs, I became aware of a small black dog around my feet.

Sometimes it was in front of me, sometimes beside; and when I turned right on Adelaide street to go along to the fishing-tackle shop, the little creature was at my heels.

I paused to look in the window of the surveyor-instrument shop. The little dog sat down.

"Hey!" I said. "I don't belong to you!"

It was a bright, eager little dog. Obviously of no particular breed. A wispy, bright sprite of a dog. And when I spoke to it, it frisked up, and its beady black eyes gleamed with affection.

"Hey, hey!" I protested. "Go and find your master."

There is nothing quite so pity-inspiring as a lost dog downtown. They look so lost, running this way and that way, dodging amidst the stupefying traffic. This little fellow, however, did not look entirely lost.

"Take a good look at me," I said. "You see I'm not the right one."

I walked along to the tackle shop.

When I pushed the door open, the little dog darted in ahead of me.

"Hello!" said the boys. "Got a dog, eh?"

6

"I've been picked up," I explained.

The little dog hustled about the tackle shop, exploring everything, meeting the boys. But it came back and sat down, very proprietorial, beside me in the chair good tackle shops provide, at this dreary season of the year, for customers to await the spring.

"What are you going to do with it?" the boys asked. "Take it home?"

"Well, no," I confessed. "We already have a dog at home."

"It has no collar and tag," they pointed out. "It's yours if you want it. It's kind of flattering to be picked up by a dog, from out of all the thousands and thousands . . ."

"Do any of you want a dog?" I suggested.

"Well, no," they said. "We've got dogs at home."

So, after a nice sit, during which spring came appreciably nearer, I prepared to leave. We prepared, I should say.

"You could take him," said the boys, "up to the Humane Society. "It's only about eight blocks from here."

"I suppose," I said.

"You could take a taxi," they added.

"Well, I've got some shopping to do up in the department stores," I reflected. "It was up around there he picked me up. Maybe he will get his bearings. If not, I will take him to the Humane Society."

So we went back around by Yonge street to the department stores, and the little dog clung right to my feet. Perish the thought, but I DID have a fleeting notion that something might distract his attention for an instant; or, that amidst all those myriad feet and legs, he might lose me. But he didn't. And when I stepped into the revolving doors of the department store, he nipped in with me, and very skilfully we both nipped out.

We had not gone far in the store, toward the fishing-tackle department, which is at the remote back end of the block, before a gentleman wearing a white carnation in his lapel to indicate he was a section manager, stopped me.

"I am sorry, sir," he said, "but it is not permitted to bring dogs in the store except on a leash or carried in the arms."

"This is not my dog," I explained. "It just picked me up on the street and is following me."

"Ah," said the manager. "In that case, we have an arrangement to have stray dogs removed. I will call one of our porters, and he will take it up to the Humane Society."

"As a matter of fact," I put in, "I was planning to take him up there myself, as soon as I have finished a little shopping."

"Ah, good," said the manager. "In that case, I will get you a bit of string."

So we put the string around the little dog's neck, and we went to the tackle department. In the big department stores, they do not provide chairs, as do the smaller tackle shops, in which to await the spring. As a matter of fact, there was no tackle I really wanted: it was just to look for a little while at all the rods in their racks, the reels, the flies, the lures. So, after a few pleasant moments, we went out to the back entrance of the big store and hailed a taxi and went to the Humane Society.

When we entered the lobby, the young lady at the switchboard called out cheerily:

"Ah, it's Pixie again!"

"Pixie?" I responded. "Pixie is a girl's name. This is a gentleman dog."

"No, if you look in the dictionary," said the young lady, "you will see there is no mention of sex. Pixie can be either."

"You know Pixie, then?"

"Indeed we do," said she. "Somebody is always bringing him in."

"What happens now?"

"We phone his owners, and they come and get him."

"This is a regular thing?"

"Yes, he comes downtown and picks somebody up and has a wonderful day of it, shopping, and getting into the most fascinating places."

"I had him in a couple of tackle shops," I admitted.

"He'd like that," agreed the young lady. "Some people apparently take him home, for he is away two or three days. But he always gets away and comes back home. He prefers shopping to the domestic life."

"Shouldn't he have a collar and tag?"

"He has," said the young lady, "but they are not too careful about putting it on him all the time."

In the Humane Society, they do have chairs in which to sit and await the spring. So I sat down for a few minutes in which to thank Pixie for having selected me out of all those thousands and thousands of legs.

And to the best of his ability, he thanked me for taking him into the tackle shops.

9

The Pin

GUESS WHO I saw downtown today!

Mutchley.

Mr. Mutchley, the schoolmaster, whose reputation I saved.

There he was, in the lobby of the Public Library, looking exactly as he did sixteen years ago. Tall, loose, bony, like a clothes horse. And his face shaved shiny and light red, as if he had been parboiled.

"Hel-LO!" I cried, holding out my hand.

He stared at me blankly.

"Clark," I said. "You remember? The pin? On the escalator?"

"Not at all!" said he, and brushed past me.

I don't see why he should feel that way about it. As a matter of fact, if it hadn't been for me he might have been in quite a predicament. I always feel I saved his reputation.

It was ten years ago. I was on the down escalator in the department store. And not because I am a nosy little guy but purely because I am a newspaperman who likes to look at everybody and everything—you know, nice and wide awake all the time—I was looking at the people coming past me on the up escalator.

And I was looking right in the face of this young

woman when she gave a wild jump forward, let out a yell, opened her mouth, bugged her eyes:

"YOW!"

You could hear it all over the crowded store. And of course everybody within sight halted and stared.

Like everybody else on the down escalator, I turned to watch back. There was the young lady turned to face the man behind her, glaring.

Just as I hit the main floor, I heard her cry:

"You stuck a PIN in me!"

Well, naturally, I hopped right on the up escalator. Who wouldn't?

By the time I got up to the next floor, there was quite a little congregation.

There was Mutchley in the middle, very flushed, his eyes starting from his head, saying over and over:

"I didn't! I wouldn't! I didn't!"

But pinning them both in the corner nearest the escalator were a number of women and men, and they didn't want to let the matter drop.

"He's one of those pinchers!" cried a short stubby little lady.

"I know the kind!" growled a heavy young man.

Fortunately at this moment a shrewd-looking lady who turned out to be one of what they call the store protective staff joined the melee. And she moved in beside the lady who had been stuck. She must have given some sort of secret signal, because promptly two store detectives arrived, in their hats and coats, looking like a couple of country cousins up for the day's shopping.

"Let's go to the office," they said.

"I didn't! I wouldn't! I didn't!" was all Mutchley could say.

"Pardon me," I said to the lady detective. "I was on the down escalator and saw the whole thing."

"Come along," said she.

Of course, I hadn't seen the whole thing. All I saw was the woman's face as she gave that violent jump and that wild yell.

But I felt it was my duty as a newspaperman to see the end of this thing.

There was, besides, something that appealed to me about Mutchley. He was one of those flushed, shiny-spectacled fellows with a natural-born look of innocence.

And it seemed to me, as we walked toward the office, that I had seen Mutchley's HAND on the rubber rail of the escalator at the very moment the girl had leaped.

They have this office for interviewing shoplifters, disorderlies and suspicious characters. And they asked us all to sit down.

The offended young lady wouldn't sit down.

"I'll STAND!" she said indignantly, glaring at Mutchley.

He must have given her a real jab.

Mutchley was glad to sit down.

First, they asked the victim to state just what happened.

She stated it in no uncertain terms. She was on the escalator. And all of a sudden, this man behind her stuck a pin into her.

"I didn't! I couldn't! I didn't!" stated Mutchley, hoarsely.

Next, they asked him his name, address and occupation. He gave it. A school teacher. Twenty years a school teacher. A respected man, with a wife and four children. Utterly unthinkable that he would do such a thing, he said.

"Ever had any trouble of this kind before?" asked one of the store detectives craftily.

"Certainly not!" said Mutchley.

"What's your age?" asked the lady detective.

"Forty-four," said Mutchley.

"Aaah!" they all said, glancing at one another.

But being safely past forty-four myself, I began to feel a growing sympathy for this tall, gangly man with the light red face and the astounded eyes.

"Now, excuse me," said I. "But I was on the down escalator at the very moment this happened. I was, indeed, just about five feet away, facing this young lady when she let out this wild yell. . . ."

"And where," asked one of the store detectives, "was this gentleman?"

"Immediately behind her," I stated, "and his right hand was on the rubber rail of the escalator!"

There was a dead silence.

"Write your name on this paper," directed one of the detectives.

Mutchley took the pencil in his left hand and wrote his name.

"Aha!" cried everybody but Mutchley and I.

"It was him!" said the young lady, slightly hysterical. "I KNOW it was him!"

I got up from my chair, since I was nearest to her.

"Now, now, my dear," I said kindly. "Here, take my chair. Do sit down!"

She sank into my chair.

"YOW!" she yelled, rising vertically about three feet in the air.

Everybody sprang to their feet, especially Mutchley.

We men were ushered out into the corridor.

The lady detective stayed behind to help investigate.

It turned out that the young victim had shortened her slip the evening before and had forgotten to take all the pins out.

One of them had got into a vulnerable position; and in her twisting in some particular fashion while on the escalator, the pin had gone home.

Apologies were general to Mutchley.

Feeling I was really responsible for his vindication, I accompanied him out into the store. But he didn't seem to realize his obligation to me. He just wanted to get free, to get the heck out of THERE.

But why should he brush me off today?

I suppose there are things you like to forget completely.

Merchandising

WHILE the boys in the wayside service station had my
carburetor assembly off trying to find out what was
giving my car the jerks, I went out to converse with the
locals. It makes me nervous to watch mechanics taking
engines apart.

There were two men sitting on the low window sill
of the service station. One was a young man nursing a
carton tied with rope. The other was an elderly man
with a battered suitcase at his feet.

Most of the traffic was up. But whenever a down car
turned in to the gas pumps, the two got up and inquired
about a lift. They were going south.

"If you're stuck," I said, when they came back to sit
after the third or fourth failure, "I'll give you a lift
when my car's ready."

They thanked me warmly, and I sat down on the
window ledge with them.

"How far are you going?" I asked.

"Well, I'm just going down about three miles," said
the young man with the carton. "Got a farm there. My
car's laid up."

"How about you?" I asked the elderly man.

"Well, no particular distance," said he. "I'm looking
for some kind of a job. So I'll drop off at one of the
towns along the way and have a look around."

The younger man laughed.

"You got a couple of problems for passengers," he said.

"Are you looking for a job too?" I asked.

"No," he said. "But see this carton? It's full of eggs. You don't need any fresh eggs, do you?"

"Well, by golly, I might take two or three dozen," I said. "What's the problem?"

"I've been up to three towns north of here this morning," said the young fellow, "trying to dispose of these eggs. But everybody's stocked up, or else they've got regular suppliers. I haven't got rid of even one dozen today."

He kicked the carton slightly.

"Is your farm on this road?" I inquired.

For traffic was quite lively, even though it was a secondary highway.

"Yes, but . . ."

"Haven't you got a fresh-egg sign out?" I asked. "On weekends you ought to do a . . ."

"I've got better than a sign out," said the young fellow. "I've got a nice gravel turn-in space, and a little shack where my young sister is ready to wait on the public. But you'll see my problem, if I get a lift with you."

Both the elderly man and I turned and looked inquiringly at him.

"My place," he said, "is at the bottom of a hill on an S turn. I'm on the right-hand side. Traffic coming down doesn't see my stand until they're practically past. And up-traffic doesn't want to stop and cross the road with that curving hill right ahead of them."

16

"Can't you move the stand farther down from the bottom of the hill?" I checked.

"No, there's a steep bank," said the young man.

The elderly man held up his hand.

"I think," he said, "I got a job!"

It was his turn to be looked at.

"Wait till I see this layout," he smiled. "But I'm old enough now to have to live by my wits. I think maybe I can help this young man."

We were still trying to discover what was in his mind when the boys came out to announce my car was all put together again and ready.

I piled my new friends in with their luggage.

Three miles down the road we came to the S turn and the hill.

"Take it slow," called the elderly man from the back seat.

I approached the lip of the hill slowly. On the right-hand side a field ended in a clump of shrubbery and bushes at the fence corner.

"Perfect!" cried the elderly man.

I coasted slowly down the S turn. As we came around the bottom turn there appeared on the right a neat spread of gravel, as large as the average service station's area; and at the back of it, a little shed with a counter in front of it, at which a young girl sat.

Conspicuously on the shed and on another white sign at the far end of the gravel were the words "Fresh Eggs."

As I turned on to the gravel, a car rushing down the hill from behind gave me a warning blast of its horn.

"See?" said the young fellow. "That's the way they go by."

The elderly man clambered out of the car, suitcase and all.

"Here," he said, "lend me that cap of yours."

The young man was wearing a hard-peaked cap of nondescript color.

"You wait here," said the elder, "and see what happens."

He put his valise in the shed, and then walked smartly back up the hill and vanished around the U turn.

"Well, well!" said I.

I put my car over beyond the shed, and the young fellow handed the carton across the counter to the girl.

Four or five cars and a truck or two came surging down the hill and scurried past.

Then came a car slowly. Not surging.

It braked at sight of us, and turned in on the gravel.

"Hello," said the young farmer, going forward.

"Er," said the driver, "could you tell me if there is a speed trap back there on the hill?"

"Speed trap?" checked the young fellow.

"Well, I was just coming to the hill," said the driver, "when I saw a man stand up in the bushes, there, with a stop-watch in his hand."

Another car came rather slowly down the hill. It went past.

But the next car drew in behind the first.

"Not that I know of," said the young farmer.

"I just caught him out of the corner of my eye," said the first driver. "He had a watch in his hand and a notebook, I think."

The newly-arrived driver got out of his car and walked **over.**

"Could you tell me," he asked, "if there's a cop at the end of that hill back there?"

We sold six dozen to the first car, four to the second.

Now that they were stopped, they might as well.

Especially if there were women passengers. They usually got out and had a look at the display of eggs, bottles of home-made maple syrup and tins of local honey the young girl was bashfully presiding over behind the counters.

I stayed an hour and a half, until the elderly man came down the hill for lunch.

They had sold twenty-one dozen eggs, six jars of syrup and four two-pound tins of local honey (last year's).

"We've got a spare room," said the young fellow to the elderly man.

"It's the kind of job I like," said the elder. "I sit on a boulder there, in the bushes. And all I do is stand up, as a car comes by, and look at my hand as if I had a watch in it."

Traffic was once more whizzing heedlessly by.

They took me back up the lane to the farmhouse for lunch.

"Actually," I said, "it's a kind of a fraud, isn't it?"

"I think it's what they call merchandising," said the elderly man, eating.

The Bonfire

FINCH, whose cottage is a little way up the beach, came up my steps. And the first thing he saw was my new tin horn hanging at the ready on the veranda wall.

"Isn't that the most ridiculous thing!" he snorted.

"Where have you got yours?" I asked.

"Just inside the screen door," said Finch. "And I've spent all afternoon preventing the children from blowing it. One of these days, some stranger is going to come on to my veranda, see the horn and give it a toot just for the fun of it. And then what happens?"

"By golly," I admitted, "the whole beach will explode into action!"

The tin horns were part of our new fire-fighting equipment that we had adopted up at the Point.

Richards, a newcomer to the beach, who had bought the old Henderson cottage, had hardly got settled around the first of July before he began agitating.

"Do you mean to say," he had demanded of us, one by one, as he made our acquaintance, "that you haven't got some kind of fire-fighting equipment up here?"

And the next thing we knew, he had started a collection of $10 from each cottage along the beach for the purpose of buying a fire pump, with one of those little engines like an outboard motor, and a length of hose sufficient to reach any of the cottages with water from its shore.

"We've relied," we told him, "on the bucket-brigade principle. Everybody along the shore has pails, and shovels for sand, and that kind of thing."

"Preposterous!" Richards had said. He is one of those authoritative executive types. "I know where we can get a second-hand outfit, as good as new. A little portable engine that you set down by the beach; a short length of hose for the intake; and three hundred feet of hose to carry a powerful stream to the scene of the fire."

"Everybody's pretty careful up here," we told him.

"Ridiculous!" said Richards.

And he took $10 off each of us.

Last week the outfit arrived, after some delay.

"It had to be overhauled and checked, you know," said Richards. "And in the middle of the season, that takes a little time."

He sent his boys along the beach to invite us all to come over after lunch and inspect the new acquisition. When we were all assembled, he stood on the steps of his veranda and addressed us.

"I have here," he said, holding up a little tin horn about a foot long, "a little article I would like to present to you all, out of my own pocket. This will be our alarm. Each cottage will have one of these horns hanging in a conspicuous place, but well out of reach of the children. In the event of fire, the first person to detect it will sound his horn. On hearing it, all the rest of us will hasten to our horns and blow them as loudly as possible. Thus, all along the beach, the alarm will be spread."

"Where will the pump be kept?" called Finch.

"In my boathouse," said Richards, magnanimously. "I have plenty of room for it. And as you know, my cottage is about at the half-way point along the beach."

We all had to admit this was generous of Richards. Most of us have no more room in our boathouses, on account of the junk that accumulates over the years.

"Tonight," went on Richards, "we are to have a rehearsal. As you can see out there on my beach, I have set up a big bonfire."

We turned and beheld a great pyramid of boughs, stumps, slabs and stuff that Richards had collected all summer off his lot, which the Hendersons had rather neglected during their occupancy.

"We will have a rehearsal," said Richards, "and in honour of the occasion, my wife is preparing refreshments for young and old, hot dogs, hamburgers, cookies and cakes, which we will all partake of after we have reduced that fire to suitable size with our pump."

We all applauded.

"Shortly after eight," said Richards, "when darkness is falling, I will light the bonfire. Whereupon, I will sound my horn."

He held up his horn.

"Each of you," he concluded, "on hearing my horn, will immediately sound his horn. And so, along the beach will spread the alarm. Then you are all to come as fast as possible. And those who are first here will assist me to carry the engine and pump out of my boathouse and get it started. By the time most of you arrive, we will be playing the hose on the fire. Not to put it out, of course. But just to reduce it a little and to demonstrate the process. We will then gather around and have a sing-song, and in due course, the refreshments. Is that clear?"

We again applauded. And Richards handed out the tin horns, one to each family.

Most of us were sitting expectantly on our veranda steps by 8 p.m., with our horns in hand.

Ten past eight, we saw the first flicker of fire from Richard's beach. Then, from house to house, we heard the blasts of the tin horns, some good, some bad, and a few extra fancy ones as the possessors tried out the possibilities of the horn. Then we all ran.

By the time I got there, a whole mob of eight or ten of my neighbours was already wrestling the pump and engine out of Richards's boathouse, with the baleful glare of the mounting bonfire throwing a dramatic light on them. Another squad was hauling out the hose and unwinding it off the reel, in readiness.

The rest of us formed a circle, a rapidly widening circle, as the crowd grew, and the bonfire mounted higher and higher. We had to draw back.

Down on the beach, we could see Richards at the pull-cord, yanking and yanking, with his helpers posed in encouraging attitudes around him.

The bonfire grew hotter. We drew back farther.

Richards yanked and yanked. Then, in the crackle and rising roar of the bonfire, we saw Richards surrender the pull-cord to one of the others around him. By this time we were all shading our eyes with our hands.

In the glare, we could see the frantic figures around the pump jumping this way and that as one after another took turns at the pull-cord.

23

Then up from the beach raced Finch.

"Buckets!" he shouted at us in the circle. "Run and get buckets! The dock's on fire."

Sure enough, sparks had ignited Richards's little wharf, which had the normal number of old oil stains on it.

We ran. We dashed in and got our buckets. We raced back. Bending free of the glare of the bonfire, we filled the buckets off the beach and doused the dock.

Then we doused the bonfire, from a discreet distance, with long throws.

When it was down to reasonable size, we all gathered round and held a sing-song, and Mrs. Richards and the ladies brought out the refreshments.

And all the time we sang, with occasional toots and obbligatos on horns, and all the time we ate, we could hear Richards, a few yards out there on the beach, still yanking and yanking.

Thruway

THE GREEN SIGN SAID: "Next exit, 22 miles." A little way beyond the sign, a pavement curved off the thruway to the right. I could see what looked like a service station some distance down the curve.

"Heck!" I said, and turned off.

All I had had for breakfast at a motel hours ago was tea, toast and some of that sinewy strawberry jam they get in pails.

"Fill 'er up," I said to the gas-station man. "Is there any good place to eat in here somewhere?"

The attendant gave the matter some thought as he hosed.

"Weeelll," he reflected, "there's a town in about five miles where there's a couple of places."

"Any good?" I inquired.

"I guess they're all about the same," said he.

"How about along on the thruway?" I asked. "Isn't there one of those good big highway restaurants along there somewhere?"

"Yes," he said. "Forty miles along there's one of them. Forty or forty-two, maybe."

"What I feel like," I informed him, "is a good tender steak. About an inch and a half thick. Not too well done. Sort of bubbling from the fire."

The attendant looked at me with new interest.

"A sirloin steak," I considered. "And a small helping of French-fried potatoes, nice and crisp, not soggy. Fresh made. You know?"

The attendant slowed the hose. You could see he was fond of food, and of thinking about it.

"Maybe, too," I added, "a side dish of sliced Spanish onion, laid out on a few leaves of lettuce. Not that head lettuce. I wouldn't eat such stuff. But real, green leaf lettuce. You know?"

The attendant wiped his mouth with the back of his free hand.

"You won't get nothing like that," he said, "around here. Not even at home."

"Forty-two miles, you think?" I queried.

"I never been there," said the attendant, "but they say it's all right."

I paid him, and drove on to the other curve back on to the thruway and gave her the gas. My stomach was grumbling.

It's a darned queer thing, I reflected, what a poor opinion most Canadians have of the cooking in their own neighbourhood.

Yes, I decided. A steak. It was nearly six hours since that skimpy breakfast, at 7 A.M. Soggy toast, tea made with lukewarm water in a pot that dribbled. And that strawberry jam! Tasting vaguely of strawberry, and full of slippery lumps of sinewy tissue, presumably berries.

A steak. About this thick. I took one hand off the wheel and showed myself how thick. An inch and a half. A sirloin.

Now, if they didn't have a charcoal broiler, I would have it pan-fried. In a dry iron pan, with nothing in it but a sprinkle of salt. Piping hot. Pan-fried. You could hear it sizzling all the way from the kitchen.

Maybe they would have one of those open kitchens, right in the wayside restaurant, where you could hear it sizzle, and smell the smoke of it.

I would sit at my table and watch the cook. I would catch his eye. When I figured it was done, I would raise my hand, with one finger, up, like this.

I took one hand off the wheel and showed myself how I would signal to the cook. One finger up, commanding. Like this.

Then, a few French fries. Maybe as many as you could hold in your two cupped hands. Not soggy, limp French fries, tasting of yesterday's fat. But crisp, gold, pale French fries, the kind that snap when you bite 'em.

And the Spanish onion! None of this chef's-salad stuff, or green salad, mixed-up odds and ends prepared early this morning by somebody just going off duty after the all-night vigil in the restaurant. No, sir! None of that soggy provender for me. Just half a Spanish onion, right out of the refrigerator, sliced thin, and spread, like playing cards fanned out, on four or maybe five leaves of beautiful dark-green lettuce leaves with curly edges, the lettuce NOT too young, but with a good, rich, ripe, faintly bitter tang to it.

Before I realized it, there was another green sign: "Twenty miles to next exit."

I slowed.

A little way off the curved side road was a gas station.

"Heck!" I said, and curved off.

"Look," I said to the attendant who came out, "is

there any kind of a GOOD eating place in along here somewhere?"

"Weeelll," he said, "there's a town in about eight miles where there's a couple of places."

"Any good?"

"I eat at home," said the attendant, who looked dyspeptic.

"How far to the big restaurant on the thruway?"

"Twenty miles or so."

"Any good?"

"From what I've heard," said he, "it's not bad."

I drove around to the other exit and got back on to the thruway.

I kept my mind off steaks by thinking about World War I and Clemenceau and Woodrow Wilson and Lloyd George, who was knock-kneed, and Earl Haig, our supreme commander, whom I never saw, though I was three years under his command. He must have been away back there, eating . . .

Far off, I saw the wayside restaurant looming on the horizon. As I drew nearer, at sixty, I could see the busy service station, the souvenir shop, the glittering array of parked cars.

I wiped my mouth with the back of my free hand.

I swept in. I parked. I strode with long strides.

I got a table. The dining room was almost deserted. It was long past two.

A startled waitress hurried to my order. She was young. She was local. She had just come on duty, after the regular waitresses had gone off.

Alas, there was no open kitchen.

I described my steak.

I showed her with my fingers, how thick. Like this.

"If there is no charcoal fire," I said, "then pan-fry it, in a piping-hot pan—an iron pan—with a sprinkle of salt on it."

I gave her complete details. The French fries. The Spanish onion. The lettuce.

She did not seem to be paying attention. She was gazing distractedly about.

Oh, you should have seen what came!

A steak, this thick! Lovely. Exactly. Bubbling from the fire. Glorious. And French fries! Thin, curved, dry, crisp, incredible.

I poised my fork.

A large dark woman came dashing from the kitchen. She swarmed to my table, snatching up the steak.

"You got the PROPRIETOR'S steak!" she gasped. And with it, vanished away.

You should have seen what *I* got.

The Cat

AS FAR, FAR back as I could remember, I had a dread of cats. Dread, I think, is the word. Not fear. Not hatred. Not revulsion. Just dread.

One time, my fishing companion, W. C. Milne, asked me to pick up his fishing tackle at his house, and gave me the key. His wife was out of town.

I didn't know the Milnes had acquired a cat. I opened the front door and started through the vestibule for the living room, where the tackle was heaped on a chair. I froze in my tracks.

Somebody was in the house!

"Margaret?" I called.

No answer.

From a golf bag in the vestibule I took an iron.

Everything in my nature told me SOMEBODY was in the house. As an old soldier, though only 30, I had an instinct for danger. I could FEEL it.

From wall to wall, I slid to the back door, finding it locked. With the niblick ready to throw or to swing, I sidled up the stairs, knowing any instant I would have to strike. In those days, I was not afraid of men.

Along the hall, into one room, then another, I moved, all tight as a stretched elastic band. In the front bedroom, on the bed was a black-and-yellow cat, arching aristocratically on being disturbed. I yelled, and chased it from the room and down the stairs and out the back door, which I opened, banging the golf stick.

"Ah, yes," said Billy Milne, when I told him. "That's our new cat."

But as I remember it, it never came home.

As a child, I used to cross the street, on my way to school, if I saw a cat in my path. In my teens, at the age when we look for chosen friends, I lost sundry friends because they had a cat in the house. In World War I, as a young fellow with the lives of thirty-eight men on my mind and soul, I led a night patrol into a ruined farmhouse and made an utter ass of myself because I let fly with a Very light pistol into a black cellar empty save for a poor mangy cat.

But I was certain it had been the enemy.

It took me weeks to restore the faith of my thirty-eight men.

Ah, cats!

"It," said my doctor friends, consolingly, "is one of those mysterious, unexplainable phobias . . . "

I was in the back half of my fifties when I visited my Aunt Minnie Greig, in Seaforth, Ont. She was my stylish aunt, a beautiful woman.

We sat on her veranda, rocking; and she, being my elder by twenty or more years, was regaling me with stories of times past.

"You were an awful little shrimp," she said.

"Was I?" I regretted.

"So timid," said Aunt Min.

"Was I?" I muttered.

"Do you remember your white cat?" she asked.

"MY white cat?" I barely whispered.

"Joe, your dad," said Aunt Minnie, rocking idly,

"bought you a white cat, since your mother wouldn't have a dog in the house. It was a beauty, that cat. Snow white."

I had a strange feeling, as I sat watching Aunt Minnie rocking, that I was in the act of taking off a heavy coat, a coat with pockets full of things.

"How old was I?" I said.

"Two," said Aunt Minnie. "You still had diapers. Do you remember what the back yard was like?"

"Yes," I said. "I was eight when we left there. There was a grape vine on the fence at the far end."

"Right," said Aunt Minnie. "A grape arbor."

"And over that fence," I said, "was Lilley's greenhouses."

"Good for you!" cried Aunt Minnie. "The Lilleys were the florists, and they had those greenhouses . . ."

"What," I interrupted cautiously, "about the cat?"

"I'm coming to that," said Aunt Minnie. "Well, the Lilleys had trouble with mice and rats in the greenhouses. So they used to put out poison."

"Did I," I asked, "like the cat? The white cat?"

"LIKE it!" cried Aunt Minnie. "There you'd go, staggering around with that cat draped over your skinny little arm."

"I . . . " I said, and stopped.

"You took the cat to BED with you," said Aunt Min. "I told your mother, Sarah Louisa, never, never to let a cat in bed with an infant. But there you were with that blamed cat on the pillow beside your head."

"Well, I . . . " I tried again, my body prickling, my back hair creeping as it did in that ruined farmhouse in Flanders.

"The cat," said Aunt Min, "seemed as attached to you as you were to it. It followed you everywhere, around the house, out the door, in the back yard."

I pressed my back against the back of my chair.

"It was white?" I asked.

"Snow white, I told you," said Aunt Min. "Well, here's what happened. Your lovely white cat disappeared!"

"Disappeared?"

"I was staying with your mother at the time," said Aunt Min. "The cat vanished. It was gone all night. It didn't come home the next day. You kept toddling around, hunting for it, upstairs, downstairs, out the door, all around the yard, back in the door, upstairs, downstairs, until we were sick of the sight of you."

"Did I cry?"

"No, you just went wandering around, looking under everything. It was kind of pitiable, really."

"So?" I said, my back no longer twitching.

"We were sitting in the kitchen, having a cup of tea," said Aunt Minnie. "Your mother, Mamie Armour, Mrs. Taylor from next door, and your Aunt Mart.

"Then," said Aunt Min, "up the back steps from the yard you came, CARRYING your white cat!"

I tightened.

"It was DEAD!" cried Aunt Min. "STIFF dead! It had been dead two days. Poisoned from Lilley's greenhouses. Its tail was sticking out stiff. Its white fur was all matted, damp. And you were HUGGING it to your little chest, your chin over it."

"What happened?" I got the question out.

"Why, we all screamed!" said Aunt Min. "Your mother was first to reach you, and she snatched the cat from you so violently, you fell back on the steps; and she THREW it half way down the yard, and we were all screaming and yelling, and Aunt Mart had a fainting spell, and you were howling, and your mother was grabbing at you . . . "

* * *

Do you know what I wish you for a Happy New Year?

I wish you the luck to find YOUR Aunt Min, and have her tell you anecdotes about your childhood.

For in them, you may find, as I found, absolution from ancient fears, and mysterious dreads, and the strange darknesses that lie beyond the horizon of consciousness.

To know is to understand, even yourself.

Hi, There!

IT IS NOW satisfactorily proven that the human race is growing taller. A scientific examination of the records of enlistment for the past one hundred and thirty years in the British, German, French and other armies reveals the indisputable fact that the average man today is two to three inches taller than the average man of a century ago.

There have been various other attempts to prove this fact. For instance, in Italy, when a few of my friends and I captured a small castle in the province of Calabria—(my friends were infantry who were carrying the elderly war correspondent along for the ride)—we found several suits of mediaeval armour in the ancestral halls. And naturally, we attempted to try them on. Being only five feet two and 17/20th inches tall, I was the only member of the party of twenty of us who could get into any one of the seven suits. These had belonged to different ancestors, as could be determined by the difference in the age and style of the armour. The mediaeval knight, in short, was a half-pint.

If we have grown two to three inches in the past century, what a pee-wee my great-grandfather should have been! But as a matter of fact, he was six feet tall and built like a bus.

I mention this merely to bring out the fact that while

the average size of the human race may be increasing, there are still likely to be plenty of shorties around for some generations to come. While the average man may be three inches taller than he used to be, the average short man is just as short as ever.

If these new statistics go unchallenged, there is a danger that industry and manufacturers generally might be carried away by them, and start putting things farther out of reach of us shorties than they are at present. Baggage racks on railroad cars, for example, are entirely useless to the average short man. Personally, I carry a walking stick at all times. My friends suppose this to be a mere affectation. It is nothing of the kind. It is to save me the indignity of having to climb up on the seats of railway coaches to retrieve my hat. I pick it down with my stick, as I often have to do off restaurant hat racks.

My stick is also handy in groceterias and self-serve emporia. While turnips, canned soup and floor wax are always within easy reach of us short people, the things we really want, such as tins of anchovies, Gorgonzola cheese and cellophane bags of those gorgeous white Texas onions, are invariably away at the back. A stick with a crook handle has many uses.

It is horrible to contemplate what will happen if the clothing industry, especially the shirt and underwear manufacturers, get hold of these new statistics and begin making shirts longer than they are now. We modest-sized men find it utterly impossible to buy a shirt that fits. Our wives always have to take a three-inch tuck in the sleeves of our new shirts. And if the neckband fits, the shirt tail hangs down below our knees. In the matter of combination underwear, if the suit fits us circumferentially, it hangs like an accordion on us vertically. That is why short men always have to undress in separate rooms from their wives, and why they always close the door while dressing in the morning for fear their children may see them in their gansies. Short men are denied the simple joy of wandering around the house of a Sunday morning in their underwear, a pleasure that other men take as a fundamental human right.

Houses are getting smaller. Sleeping car berths, as anybody who has ridden in the new roomette cars can testify, are contracting. Automobiles, under the influence of these little English cars, are being condensed, in defiance of the new scientific statistics about the growth of our species. That is no skin off us shorties' noses.

We have just one little question to ask these busybodies who went about exploring the enlistment records of the armies of the past:

Why didn't they include the hat measurements in their inquiries? You average people who are on the rise might like to know that we shorties still wear the same size shoes and hats.

It is only in between that we lag.

Squid

"I'M HAVING the usual group," said my neighbour Davis, "over tomorrow, around five for the usual international barbecue. You'll come?"

"Delighted," I said. "What is it to be this year?"

"Chinese," said Davis.

Last year, it was Arab. Davis is our champion back-yard barbecue artist. From his garden, all summer long, there waft up the most remarkable odours. He is not one of these timid fellows who trundle out a black tin barbecue every now and then and burn up a few steaks or chops. Davis loves back-yard cookery, and spends more on the gadgetry of the barbecue than most men spend on golf. It is his hobby.

"Chinese?" I questioned. "Does it lend itself to the barbecue?"

"Chinese cookery," stated Davis, "is, without question, the finest in the world. And in China, it is almost universally done on charcoal."

"I remember last year," I said. "Those skewers you gave us, three feet long, with things blazing on them . . .

"That was Arab cookery," explained Davis. "It, also, is the finest cookery in the world. It also is done on charcoal. Those were shishkabobs or shashliks you had last year."

"I remember them well," I assured him. "Small comfortable bite-size chunks of lamb interspersed on the skewer with a quarter tomato, a mushroom, a lamb's kidney."

"A chunk of onion," put in Davis.

"Ah, yes," I said. "The onion. I thought perhaps the lamb's kidney was a little under-done."

"I worked too fast last year," confessed Davis. "When I saw the first of you walking around the garden with those blazing skewers of food, I tried to hurry it, so that we could all wander around with blazing skewers."

He wiped the back of his hand across his mouth at the mere recollection of them.

"Tomorrow," he said, "it will be Chinese. When you come into the garden, you will see all the ingredients set out on the trestle table I have ready. They will be raw. In a matter of minutes, such is the genius of Chinese cooking, you will be eating them, piping hot, crisp, crunchy . . ."

"That's what I like about Chinese food," I admitted. "All sorts of flavours, all sorts of textures."

"That's it!" cried Davis. "Texture, colour, flavour! The Chinese know how to present food to your appetite. For example, one of the things you are having tomorrow night is squid."

"Squid?" said I.

"Yes, squid, or cuttlefish," said Davis. "A great delicacy not only in China, but celebrated in the Mediterranean countries. It has a very curious and exciting flavour. In texture, it is chewy. For example, in the chow mein I am preparing tomorrow, you will one moment be chewing a crisp, nutty slice of water chestnut, or a rich, melting mouthful of chicken liver. But the very NEXT bite will be on a morsel of squid. Chewy, elusive, slippery to your teeth, with a strange, musky, yet delicate and elusive flavour, as elusive as the texture."

"I'll be there," I assured him.

And I was. By 5:15 next afternoon, all twelve of us guests were assembled in the Davis garden. The barbecue fires, two of them, were glowing cherry red, already showing the lacy grey so perfect for the culinary art.

In front of the barbecues, Davis had the long trestle table loaded with large platters of bean sprouts, which he bought, of course, in the can; green and white Chinese lettuce; heaps of water chestnut and bamboo shoots; large long-handled frying pans filled with the meaty ingredients of chow mein, chicken, chicken livers, shredded pork, black mushrooms, egg noodles, celery, strips of mango.

And in a glass dish, all by itself, the squid.

"Ladies and gentlemen," said Davis, adjusting his tall white chef's hat, "your attention, please."

And as we gathered in front of the table, he lifted the squid out of the dish and held it aloft for our inspection. It was a limp, horrifying spectacle, a bell-shaped object with tentacles dangling from it wetly.

"Now, now!" protested Davis, as we recoiled with "ughs" and "euchs." "Wait till you see what I do with it. This is the true, inward genius of Chinese cuisine. They can take the unlikeliest things, 100-year-old eggs, bird's nests, shark fins, dried ducks, and all the weird and gruesome objects you see hanging in a Chinese grocery window, and with them concoct masterpieces of gastronomy that are the wonder of the world."

He plopped the squid down on a wooden chopping

board, took a small nickel-plated cleaver such as they sell at barbecue outfitters', and with a few deft strokes chopped the squid, tentacles and all, into small pieces.

Before our admiring gaze, he slurped a dash of peanut oil into this frying pan, a handful of Chinese greens into another, a panful of bean sprouts into a third. In no time at all, such a fragrant steam was rising about us that we all stepped forward to the trestle table and helped ourselves to plates, knives, forks and spoons; and a couple of us to chopsticks.

Davis was like a whirling dervish for a few minutes, keeping no fewer than six frying pans jumping on, off, on again, over the shadowy red of the charcoal, giving this one a shake, that one a toss. He was a veritable Leonard Bernstein conducting a chow mein.

"Bung ho!" he cried, lifting the first of the pans.

And we filed past him as he ladled the contents of pan after pan on to our plates, chow mein, Chinese greens, won ton, foo yung, squares of pineapple, strips of mango, heaps of noodles dry, or noodles wet.

And a bowl of rice for every guest.

To the chairs set ready for us in the garden, we retreated. Davis was the last to be seated.

"Now," he cried for our attention, "let me know when you get a bit of squid. It's there somewhere. You will detect the delicate, exotic flavour, the curious chewy texture, in such contrast to the slices of water chestnut."

"I got one," said our neighbour, Simpson.

He chewed. He chewed and chewed.

We all watched.

He swallowed.

In due time, we all got some squid. We chewed.

"It tastes," I suggested, "sort of like rubber."

41

"Right!" said Davis. "And the texture?"

"Rubbery," I admitted.

There was a consensus. Squid feels and tastes like rubber.

"It's exotic," said Davis, sweeping up the chow mein with chopsticks. He is an expert. And he chewed and chewed, with half-shut eyes.

And when it was all done and we sat back and agreed that this was the best international barbecue yet, we all got up and helped Mrs. Davis and the girls red up the table.

"Hey!" said Davis. "Where's the elastic band off the butter jar?"

"What elastic band?" asked Mrs. Davis.

"That big thick elastic band," said Davis, "that I had around the wax paper on top of the butter jar."

"The last I saw it," said Mrs. Davis, "it was on that chopping board."

"Dear me!" said Davis, glancing wide-eyed around the whole company.

The Call

"BETTY CARTER phoned," announced my women-folk as I hung up my hat and coat.

"Aha!" I said. "I wonder what she's up to?"

"It's about some birds she saw at her feeding tray in the garden," explained my womenfolk.

But I had my suspicions. Betty Carter is always playing tricks on her Uncle Greg and Aunt Helen. She is a marvellous mimic.

Sometimes she is one of these telephone soliciting agents, asking what time they are to pick up our rugs to be cleaned. She can affect the nippy, clipped tone of a telephone girl to perfection. And there we are hollering all over the house to find out who ordered the rugs to be picked up.

That's simple. But sometimes she will be the Duchess of Patoot, by the sound of her, announcing that she is the chairman of the Ladies International Peace On Earth, Good Will Towards Men Society, and inviting Uncle Greg to address the March meeting of the society, or maybe requesting Aunt Helen to pour tea. Betty Carter can sound so convincing that I have been known to accept speaking engagements to the Canadian Bankers' Association.

"Birds!" I said, sniffing, as I came out of the hall coat closet. "What kind of birds?"

"She said," reported my womenfolk, "they were about the size of baked Idaho potatoes . . ."

"Oh, yeah?" I commented.

"And kind of yellowy, buffy, Chinese printy sort of . . ."

"By golly!" I said, as I proceeded upstairs. "Evening grosbeaks! What's Betty's number?"

"It's on a bit of paper on your desk," called my womenfolk.

Evening grosbeaks!

This was exciting news. If Betty Carter had evening grosbeaks at her feeding station, it wouldn't take me long to hop in the car and drive out to the suburb where she lives.

I wouldn't miss a chance to see these ravishing birds. True, they are so chunky they might suggest a sort of baked Idaho potato, for size. But, oh, how beautiful they are in the light of a winter afternoon. A strange dusky yellow, soft and shadowy like old parchment, with curious patterned blotches of white and black on wings and tail, and a bright yellow eye-brow on the male. Their beaks are huge and ivory-coloured. And as they feed so tamely—you can approach within a few feet of them, they are such innocent strangers from the far north, coming down here for the winter—you can appreciate how like a beautiful Japanese or Chinese print they are. Seeing them is like hearing a perfect sound of music, a few-times-in-a-lifetime thing.

I found the scrap of paper on my desk with the telephone number on it.

"Hello!" said a rich contralto voice when I dialled.

"Hi, Betty!" I laughed. For I knew she had been waiting for me.

"Whom," said the voice, "did you wish to speak to?"

"I hear you've got some birds," I cut through her disguise.

"Birds?" said she.

"Go ahead, darlin'," I said. "If they're what I think they are, I'll be over in thirty minutes."

"I'm afraid," went the voice, and I was astonished at the depth and vibrato she was getting into it, "you are labouring under some mistake. Who is speaking? And what are you speaking in connection with?"

"By golly, Bett," I cried, "you sound like an Anglican archdeacon! It's terrific!"

(We have some Anglican archdeacons in the family, though not on our Presbyterian side.)

To my complete consternation, Betty hung up abruptly.

Three or four of my womenfolk had come upstairs, and a few of them looked in the door of my den.

"What did she say?" they asked.

"She hung up," I said, puzzled. "Maybe it wasn't Betty, after all."

Maybe I had the wrong number.

So, holding the scrap of paper before my eyes, I redialled it carefully.

The same rich voice answered.

"Hello?"

"Is that not Mrs. Carter's residence?" I inquired.

"It is NOT!" replied the voice, instantly clacking down the receiver.

Well, my womenfolk are pretty good at taking down numbers a little off register. So I looked up Betty's number in the phone book. It bore no resemblance.

"Hi, Betty!" I hailed heartily, when Betty herself answered in her very own voice.

45

"You're too late," she announced. "I had over twenty evening grosbeaks at the feeding tray an hour ago."

"Aw, heck!" said I.

"If they come back," she said, "I'll ring you the minute I see them . . ."

And she then regaled me with a most fascinating account of how the grosbeaks looked, four males, seven females, and the rest immatures of the first winter.

So when we had finished talking about the grosbeaks, I hung up and took the scrap of paper with the phone number on it down to show my womenfolk how it bore no earthly resemblance to Betty's number, and in future, would they be so kind as to exercise a little care in noting down telephone numbers.

"Oh, that?" they said, when I exhibited the bit of paper. "That's another number. That's Archdeacon Somebody who . . ."

"WHAT!" I yelled, agonized.

"Archdeacon Somebody or other," they said. "He telephoned just after you went out . . ."

"Oh, nooooooo!" I moaned.

"He wanted to invite you to address a society; it sounded like the Peace On Earth, Good Will Towards Men, or something like that . . ."

So after supper, when my fishing partner, W. C. Milne, happened by, I got him to call Archdeacon Somebody. Milne's voice isn't anything like mine. I got him to pretend he was Gregory Clark; and when the Archdeacon issued the invitation, Milne explained that he was unable to accept any speaking engagements for the next few months due to absences from town and previous commitments.

But things can get very confusing, can't they?

Uncle Earl

WE WERE well into our lunch when Herriot appeared in the restaurant, looking excited.

"Guess what!" he exclaimed as he sat down at the table. He didn't wait for us to guess.

"The Marks pond," he whispered, glancing around to make sure there were no eavesdroppers, "the Marks pond is up for lease!"

We all stopped chewing and stared at him in unbelief.

"It's true!" said Herriot. "I just met old Mr. Winters on the street. He told me that he and the two old boys who have had the lease for thirty-five years have decided to give it up."

We all swallowed and forgot to eat.

"He wrote Mr. Marks, the farmer, only yesterday," said Herriot. "So, by golly, if we make it fast, maybe we can get up there in time to take over the lease."

This was sensational news. The Marks farm is only forty miles from the city, less than an hour's drive. It is in a sequestered little valley three miles in from the highway. It lies snug and secure, far from the madding crowd. And on that farm is the most beautiful, fertile, abundant little trout pond in all creation.

"We'll go tonight!" I declared. "Right after five!"

"We'll be there by six," agreed Cooper. "He would

47

only have got the letter today. He wouldn't have time to offer it to anybody."

"Make it four!" said Herriot, waving the waitress away. "We can all duck out of the office by four."

"We had better take some money," Cooper suggested. "If the four of us bring $25 each, that'll be a hundred we can plunk down to clinch the deal."

"Right!" said Herriot. "I asked old Mr. Winters what they had been paying, and he said $200 a year."

"That would be fifty bucks from each of us," figured Cooper. "And where could you get a year's recreation? . . ."

We never even finished our coffee.

At 4:15 we were car-borne.

At 5:15 we were turning off the highway on to the gravel road that leads to the Marks farm.

At 5:30 we were entering the lane. When we pulled up beside the farmhouse, there was the fabled Marks pond one hundred yards down the slope, in full view of the house, and safe from poachers day and night the whole year round. What an investment!"

Herriot was first out, and it was he who rapped on the door. We had appointed him spokesman, and given him the money.

"Mr. Marks?"

"Yes."

An elderly man in his pants and undershirt, his suspenders hanging, stood sleepily in the doorway.

"We understand the pond is up for lease," said Herriot, as we all drew near.

"I believe it is," said Mr. Marks, patting his thin hair back and rubbing his eyes. He had obviously been roused from a snooze.

"May we come in," asked Herriot, "and discuss the terms on which we might lease it?"

"Why, certainly, certainly," said Mr. Marks. "Come right in."

The kitchen was spotless. African violets bloomed in profusion on window sills. Mr. Mark's indicated chairs, and we drew them up around the kitchen table.

"What would you say," opened Herriot, "to $200 for the year, the same as Mr. Winters and his friends have been paying?"

"It sounds reasonable," said Mr. Marks.

Herriot drew from his pocket the tens and fives, and counted them on to the table.

"There's one hundred down," said he, "to seal the deal."

Mr. Marks looked intently at the money, reached out and took it; and after pocketing it in his trousers, accepted Herriot's proffered hand, and then shook hands all around.

"Well, that's that," said Herriot.

We all felt a little flattened by the ease and informality with which this wonderful transaction was concluded.

"We'll go down now," I suggested, "and have a look at the pond?"

"By all means," said Mr. Marks, retiring.

In radiant spirits, we walked down the slope to the edge of the pond. We stood on the small plank wharf and peered into the beautifully clear water. Cooper lifted an old board and nabbed a couple of worms from under it. These he tossed out into the pond. Instantly, the water humped and swirled as trout surged up and snatched the worms. We were bewitched.

We walked around the margin, ducking under the fragrant cedars that hemmed the edges. At the far end was another rustic wharf built out thirty feet into the pond. We were all on it, almost speechless with joy at the prospect of opening the season next Saturday, when a car drove up alongside ours, away over by the farmhouse, and a man and two women got out of it. They stood looking at us for a moment and then went indoors.

After another twenty minutes of gloating exploration, we rounded the far side and came back up the hill to the farmhouse.

"We'll say good-bye," said Herriot, rapping at the door.

A stranger opened.

"Ah," said Herriot, "could we say good-bye to Mr. Marks?"

"I'm Mr. Marks," said the stranger.

"Oh," said Herriot, "I mean the Mr. Marks we dealt with regarding leasing the pond."

"I'm the Mr. Marks you deal with in leasing the pond," said he.

"But . . ." said Herriot.

"Come in," said Mr. Marks.

We all trooped in. The ladies, Mrs. Marks and Miss Marks, were introduced to us.

"There's some mistake," began Herriot. "When we arrived here, an hour ago, we met a Mr. Marks . . ."

"That would be my brother," said Mr. Marks.

"Uncle Earl," said the two ladies.

"And after discussing with him," continued Herriot, "the fact that Mr. Winters had told us he was giving up the lease, we closed the deal with him, and gave him $100."

Mr. Marks, Mrs. Marks and Miss Marks stood stiff still. The clock ticked.

Suddenly, as one, they whirled and dashed out of the kitchen, down the hall. There was a long silence. Then they all returned.

"He's gone!" said Mr. Marks.

"His valise is gone, too!" said Mrs. Marks.

"Good riddance," said Miss Marks, "to bad rubbish!"

"Gentlemen," said Mr. Marks, "my brother turned up here last summer, and has been with us ever since. A lazier man I never knew. We didn't know how to get rid of him. You have provided the means. Therefore, I tell you what I'll do. I got Mr. Winter's letter this morning. I'll lease you the pond for $200. I'll consider $100 already paid."

"Thank heavens!" said Mrs. Marks.

"Glory be!" said Miss Marks.

"You gentlemen owe me $100," said Mr. Marks. "And you can pay it next week, when, I presume, you will be coming up here to open the trout season."

"I'll have supper on in half an hour," said Mrs. Marks. "Hang up your hats, and make yourself to home."

The Talisman

NUMBERS of people who have seen me in my underwear or with my shirt collar ajar have been curious about a small stone with a hole in it that I wear on a fishline around my neck.

Well, I'll tell you.

My Grandma, Louisa Greig (née McMurray), was a quiet, soft-spoken woman who begat seven vociferous children, three boys and four girls.

By the time I became truly aware of her, when I was eight or nine years old, these children of hers were adults, and Grandma Greig sat aside amidst the tumult of them, and did nothing much but smile.

They gave her a footstool covered with dark red Brussels carpet. And when she put her chubby little feet on it, in their elastic-sided shoes, there was just room for me.

And there I could sit, hour after hour, not talking much, nor asking many questions, but just looking up at her smile and trying to learn how not to be vociferous.

It was the kind of friendship that does not require much conversation. Sometimes Grandma Greig would not speak at all for fifteen minutes. And I would not interrupt her.

"Greg," she said to me one day, "if ever you find a little stone with a hole in it, tie it around your neck."

"What will that do, Grandma?"

"It will protect you from the arrow that flieth by day," she said, "and the pestilence that walketh in darkness."

I was twenty-five years old before I found the little stone.

But of course I hunted in between. For instance, Dr. Mills, who lived down the street, had a gravel lane leading into his stable where he kept his horse and dogcart. And the very day that Grandma gave me the prescription, I went immediately to Dr. Mills's lane, and sorted over 200,000 pebbles before supper time. Without luck. On my way to school, I would sometimes see the roofing men, with their steaming tank of tar on wheels, and a wagonload of gravel; and I would cautiously sift through the gravel with my fingers until told to run along. Each summer, for three or four years, until I grew up to the manhood of twelve or fourteen, I remembered Grandma Greig, and would walk the long washed beaches, and go over the stones, all in vain.

But gradually, while I did not forget her, I was able to see gravel on the roadsides and even on great beaches without getting down on hands and knees to search. The Battle of Vimy was over, and I was on ten days' leave to England, and all my life had changed, and Grandma Greig was like a song or a poem out of olden time. I reached London on a Saturday night from France. And Sunday morning, I got up early in the Strand Palace Hotel (officers, bed and breakfast, six and six, on the top floor. The Zeppelins were about, and the top floors of hotels were cheap to the military).

Like Yonge street in Toronto, you could shoot a cannon up the Strand on a Sunday morning and not hit a soul.

But I had hardly walked a block in that vast quiet city before I came face to face with Col. John Malloch of the Medical Corps, home from Salonika. And he told me No. 4 Canadian General Hospital, of which he was then officer commanding, was also home from Salonika, and stationed at Basingstoke.

And this meant that my boyhood and young-manhood closest buddy and fishing companion, Staff Sgt. Billy Milne, M.S.M., was here in England with it.

I hadn't seen or heard from him in two years.

From Col. Malloch, there on the Strand, I got a pass written out on a scrap of paper for Staff Sgt. Milne. And down to Basingstoke I went on the first train. In my best old infantry manner I saw the adjutant of the hospital, presented the pass; and Staff Sgt. Milne handed over his duty to his next in line.

"When's the next train to London?" I asked Billy.

"To Brighton, you mean," said Billy. "Woody McKeown is there at the Old Ship. He's on leave too!"

Now, this sort of thing doesn't happen except in books. Woody McKeown was the third of the triumvirate of Milne, Clark and McKeown.

"He's a captain," said Billy, "transferred to the British artillery."

So down to Brighton go Lt. Clark and Staff Sgt. Milne to the Old Ship Hotel.

Though it was Sunday, and after noon, the bar down

the cellar was open; and there sat Capt. Woody McKeown, of the British artillery, talking Limey, like an old-timer, with a couple of other Limeys, nosing into a mug of mild and bitter.

When the shouting died, Woody and Billy and I went for a promenade to lay plans for the Conquest of London.

And along the promenade, we saw, despite the war, thousands of people on the shore, and swimming.

Billy and Woody, being athletes, insisted on a swim. But after one look at the dirty, scummy, seaweedy waters of Brighton, I said to heck with it. I sat on the beach.

On the beach I sat and watched my two closest friends, here in this far country, in these shattered years, now miraculously brought together out of all the millions of men.

And as I watched them horsing around in the sea, I heard across the sunlit Channel the sound Brighton knew well, the remote mutter and quiver of the guns in France. It was half sound, half vibration.

I said to myself:

"When will we three meet again?"

I lowered my glance between my knees, on to the sea-washed gravel of Brighton.

Straight, straight as a needle, into the eye of the hole in a little pebble.

As if it were this morning, not forty-four years ago, I remember the tingle that went from my heels up and down my bent legs and up my back to burst like one of those skyrockets.

I stared at the pebble quite a long time before picking it up. I half expected it to vanish. It was smaller in diameter than a penny.

I picked it up, rose and walked up the gravel slope to the bathing huts, where an old man in a sailor cap rented them.

"Have you got a bit of fish line?" I asked.

I tied it around my neck.

Each time I change the cord, I put the new cord through before cutting the old. It has been on my neck forty-four years.

Oh, yes, we three met again! Milne came safe home to a career in industry; Woody McKeown to a career in law, ending up a magistrate of the City of Toronto.

But that isn't it.

In all the long years, no arrow that flieth by day has found me, and no pestilence that walketh in darkness.

That was Grandma Greig's promise, and it was kept.

Yoo-hoo!

"YOO-HOO, Mr. Clark!" called Mrs. Gadsby from her back steps. "Yoooooo-hoo!"

But I kept right on running.

The bus was only half a block away.

"Yoo-hooooo, Mr. Clark!" shrilled Mrs. Gadsby, jumping up and down and waving.

I waved back at her, on the gallop.

"Later!" I shouted.

I just made it to the bus stop, a little breathless as I boarded.

Mrs. Gadsby is a charming neighbour, and a friendlier one you couldn't wish for over the fence.

But she DOES want to tell me the latest about her granddaughter aged fourteen months. Yet when I try to tell her the latest about my grandson, aged fifteen months, she interrupts me right at the punch line, with another about her granddaughter.

Anyway, this was no time for anecdotes about grandchildren. I was in a spot. It was exactly 12:12 P.M. by my watch, as I sank into the bus seat. If I didn't get back to the house by 1 P.M. sharp the gang would go on without me. That was the agreement. If I wasn't on my front steps, packed and ready, at 1 P.M. sharp, it meant I wasn't coming.

Not coming? On the first day of the duck season?

With Herriot, Cooper, my brother Art and Dr. Secord?

And Dr. Secord's famous black Labrador retriever?

And the five of us, by special invitation, to one of the greatest private duck marshes in the whole country?

Do you think I'm crazy?

But I had to have my gun. And early this morning, when I was packing my gear before leaving for the office, I had made the shocking discovery that my old double-barrelled shotgun had a broken spring in the front trigger.

So I took it downtown with me and left it at the gunsmith's.

He not only promised to have it ready by noon, but said he would have one of his clerks take it up to my place at noon exactly, and be sitting on my front steps waiting for me.

Never leave your gun to the last minute. I always say, take your gun out two weeks before the season opens and examine it carefully. And that, of course, is what I did. But it may have been the way I was snapping it at imaginary flights of black ducks up there in my attic store room that broke the spring.

And another thing. Never leave it to any gunsmith to deliver your gun the day before the season opens.

There was no clerk sitting on my steps when I rushed home at exactly noon. (My family were all away.)

So I dashed in and telephoned the gunsmith. Line busy.

I ran to the front door and left it open, so that if the boy came, he would know I was in.

I phoned again. Line busy.

"Taxi!" I decided. And telephoned the taxi.

Line busy.

It was 12:08.

It might take a taxi 10 or 15 minutes to get here.

If I took a bus down, I could easily catch a taxi at the stand on the next corner from the gunsmith's.

Out of the door I raced, seeing the bus half way down the block. Twelve-eleven.

"Yoo-hoo!" Mrs. Gadsby had cried.

I burst open the gunsmith's door at precisely 12:39.

Everybody but Sandy, the old handyman, was out to lunch. Sandy is deaf.

"My gun!" I yelled.

"The boy took it," said Sandy. "He's sitting on your steps."

"He ISN'T!" I shouted.

"Left here at eleven," said Sandy. "Saw to it myself."

"It doesn't take twenty minutes to my place!" I cried.

"Told him to sit right on your steps," said Sandy.

"Which boy was it?" I asked.

"Louis, the good one," said Sandy.

At that moment, Louis walked in the door.

"My gun, my gun!" I wailed, noting he was empty-handed.

"I was sitting there," said Louis, "when the lady over the fence said to leave it with her."

"Ooooo!"

"She was right in her garden, and said she would see you come home."

It was now 12:43.

Out the door and down to the taxi stand on the double.

No taxis.

"There'll be one here any minute," said a man sitting on a kitchen chair.

There wasn't one for four minutes.

"Make it fast," I cried, "and there's an extra buck in it!"

It was now 12:48.

Surely the boys would wait five minutes? Ten minutes?

Not that I am a duck hunter. I can't hit them. I always shoot where they were, not where they are.

But when you go with people like Dr. Secord and my brother Art, you never come home without ducks. And naturally, nobody asks you if you shot them yourself. What a question!

Twelve-fifty-two, a stop light.

Twelve-fifty-seven, another stop light.

One!

P.M.

Around the last corner, at 1:04, I craned to see if there was a station wagon parked in front of my door.

There wasn't.

I paid the taxi driver the fare and gave him the buck for luck.

"Yoo-hooo, Mr. Clark!" came Mrs. Gadsby's voice from her back steps.

I ran to the fence.

She was holding up my gun case and waving it at me.

"Yoo-hoo!" she said, coming down to bring it to me.

"Mrs. Gadsby," I called eagerly, "was there a station wagon in front of my . . . ?"

"Yes, there was," said Mrs. Gadsby. "It was there about ten to one, and then it drove off not more than two minutes ago."

She hoisted my gun case over the fence to me.

"Yoo-hoo, Mrs. Gadsby," I said hollowly.

But she knew I meant to say thank you.

The Sullen One

NEAR 5 P.M., the bus was pretty crowded. But I got a place at the back, where the seats are like benches and face each other.

Opposite me sat a sullen woman. She was well-dressed. The small parcels she held in her gloved hands were fancy-paper tied ones that come from classy shops. A well-to-do woman between fifty and sixty.

But a more sullen, sulkier expression you would seldom see in private, let alone in public. I don't know about you. But as a newspaperman, I take great interest in the people to be seen everywhere. Maybe ninety-nine out of one hundred of us could not describe one person among all the fellow passengers with whom we came home in bus or train tonight. Newspapermen live by people. We not only have to count upon them for stories. They are readers. And we have to try to fathom our readers.

I sure hoped this woman didn't read me. Her mouth was moulded in permanent lines of sulkiness. There was a contemptuous set to her lips. Her eyes wore a veiled expression, as if she were blind to all around her. She was withdrawn.

Maybe, I thought, *she is not accustomed to riding in buses or other public conveyances. Possibly she rides in a chauffeur-driven limousine!*

Our end of the bus was full of interesting types. She

ignored them all. Two other women with arms full of parcels and mouths full of chatter. Two pretty girl students, arms full of books, sitting gravely in scholarly silence. A fine old man with a stick that had a large rubber cap on the tip; probably lame. A thin man with the sniffles, avidly reading the sports pages which he turned wide-armed, to the inconvenience of his seat mates, of whom he was oblivious. Interesting, human beings.

But the sullen one was unaware of everything, everybody. I got my eye on her and couldn't take it off.

Somewhere I had seen a face like hers in a painting, or a bust of statuary. Was it a bust of Voltaire? Or Nero? In my travels, I had seen a countenance as devoid of human compassion as hers, maybe in one of the galleries in Florence. I could not recall.

Possibly she became aware of my attention, for her mouth set in more morose lines than ever, and for a fleeting instant I thought I caught a malevolent flash of dark, sombre eyes.

Pity, I said, *her husband, her children. Imagine an embittered, cross-grained woman like this in the house! Sure, she may have had griefs, tragedies ...*

At which moment, there was a loud bang underneath us, the rear end of the bus.

We had left the downtown district and were threading the crowded uptown thoroughfares full of home-goers.

All of us started at the bang. The two chatty women gave small exclamations. The sniffler looked up sharply from his paper. The old man with the rubber-tipped cane half rose from his seat.

"Backfire!" I announced cheerily.

62

We all relaxed. The sullen woman roused herself from her abstraction to turn and glance out the window behind her.

She was the first to stand up.

The driver up front had stopped the bus and flung his doors open. He leaped up and called back to us:

"It's the electric pump! No cause for alarm, folks, but if you'll just kindly leave the . . ."

Smoke was whirling up past our windows as he called, and a sudden pandemonium broke loose among us. The two chatty women, with shrill screams, were up and shoving. The thin sniffling man threw his paper aside and tried to break past them. I don't know, honestly, what I was intending to do. But whatever it was, I was halted instantly by a voice.

"Now, my dears, take it easy! There is no cause for panic."

The voice was a clear, commanding contralto, with authority in it, and assurance, and a weird and mystical calm.

Up front, passengers nearest the front exit were plunging and shoving. Smoke was already seeping hazily into the bus. But at the rear exit, those from the back and those nearest the exit from the middle of the bus, had formed a solid mass of frozen-faced, shoving, immovable humanity.

"If you will take it easy," rang the lovely voice, "and assist one another . . ."

It was the sullen woman. Her lips were parted, her eyes alive and she was transfigured.

"Sir, if you will step inside the seat, there, and let the young lady pass you . . ."

We all stilled. The haze of smoke was thicker. The

clatter, shake and thump of the departing passengers eased up. We relaxed.

The two chatty women had got out, parcels and all. The sniffling man was gone. The two young students, arms full of books and a little white of face and large of eye, stood silently to let the old man with the cane limp ahead.

The bus emptied quietly, orderly, in less than thirty seconds.

I stood aside to let the sullen one precede me.

"Thank you," she smiled.

Outside, the driver was squirting his fire extinguisher under the rear end.

"It's O.K.!" he said. "It's nothing. These darn electric pumps . . ."

We stood in a huddle, all feeling a little embarrassed with one another. Some of us quietly beat it. Others began asking the driver if he was to continue, or would he give us transfers so we could take another bus without having to pay. The street traffic that had halted and piled up to watch the excitement, began moving off. The two girl students came and stood with their arms full of books quite close to the tall, sullen woman and were venturing a few words with her.

Her face was beautiful in the light of the street lamps as she replied to the girls. They formed a little cluster of beauty in the dark tumbled street scene.

I edged over to them.

"Madam," I said, "I wish to beg your pardon."

"Whatever for?" she asked.

I lifted my hat and walked away, and unless she reads this, she will never know why I begged her pardon.

64

Mucketty-hi-ki

SHORTLY after 6 A.M. I heard our garbage-pail cover go clank in the side entrance.

I leaped out of bed and stuck my head out the window.

There was Mucketty-hi-ki, head high, tail over his back, proud and haughty even in shameful flight, hustling out our side drive.

"Hyaaaahh!" I sent after him.

He never deigned to glance back, never even hastened his mincing, proud gait.

A window slid open across the street. It was my neighbour Thompson.

"Who was it?" he called softly, so as not to rouse the whole neighbourhood at this early hour.

"Mucketty-hi-ki," I replied.

"That darn dog!" said Thompson, bitterly.

Ours is a blind street, twenty houses to the side. At the top, its fine stone wall barring all farther progress, sits the home of Mrs. McNulty, our well-to-do and aristocratic neighbour, who sets the tone of the whole street.

She is the owner of Mucketty-hi-ki, the Pekinese, who is a thorn in all our flesh.

He is the apple of Mrs. McNulty's eye, the darling of her heart. He weighs about eight pounds. Though none of us has ever been in Mrs. McNulty's home, the rumour is pretty well established that Mucketty-hi-ki has a crib that sits beside Mrs. McNulty's bed, and blue and white silk-bound coverlets tuck the little demon in.

Little demon I say, advisedly. In the thirty-nine houses of our street there are eighteen dogs and seven cats. The dogs range from cocker spaniels of various ages, sizes and colours, through boxers, dachshunds, a large collie, pronounced "coalie," and three or four nameless but none the less happy mutts.

And Mucketty-hi-ki has cowed them all.

It is an absurd sight to see Laddie, the big eighty-pound collie, slink respectfully to one side, tail between his legs, when Mucketty-hi-ki comes proudly down the street. Those who saw the one and only altercation between Laddie and Mucketty-hi-ki declare that Mucketty-hi-ki bit Laddie in a very unsportsmanlike place.

Laddie isn't the only one. Every dog and cat on the street seems to acknowledge Mucketty-hi-ki as king.

It was last spring, however, that we began to realize that Mucketty-hi-ki is not so much king of the street, as gang leader. A sort of Al Capone.

On garbage day, half the garbage cans on the street would be overturned. It took us some time, and considerable watching from behind curtains, to establish the fact that Mucketty-hi-ki was actually going and inviting larger dogs to come with him, to overturn the cans. Then Mucketty-hi-ki made them all stand back while he explored the contents.

When we tactfully telephoned Mrs. McNulty and suggested she keep the little dog on her own property on garbage days, she was furious. Did we think, she demanded, that a tiny dog like Who Flung Dung, or whatever his Chinese name is, could overturn garbage cans?

The Lavenders have two Siamese cats. Mrs. Lavender never, never lets them out in her garden unaccompanied. You can imagine Mrs. Lavender's feelings when one day Mucketty-hi-ki came tippy-toe in the side drive, and before Mrs. Lavender could say shoo, the little devil had yapped the two precious Siamese up an elm tree. Then out the drive he pranced, gave his gang call, a rather high-pitched yap with curious overtones, and summoned six of his gang, including Laddie, two spaniels, the boxer, and two mutts. And pandemonium reigned in the Lavenders' yard until she went screaming out on the street and summoned all the housewives to come and capture their dogs.

When they called on Mrs. McNulty that afternoon, a delegation of four of our ladies, she received them in state like Queen Victoria, in whose reign Mrs. McNulty was born.

She served them tea in Royal Doulton.

"Ladies," she said, after listening with amused contempt to the recital of Mucketty-hi-ki's misdemeanours over the past months, "ladies, I paid $750 for this beautiful little creature in Baltimore. He comes of royal lineage. His ancestors were known as the Lion Dogs."

"He is a gangster," whispered Mrs. Lavender.

"When the British," went on Mrs. McNulty, "looted the Imperial Palace in Peking in the year 1860, they found four of these wonderful little dogs hidden behind royal tapestries. No one in the world owned a Pekinese save the Emperor of China. The British brought the four to England. One was presented to Queen Victoria. The other three were taken by the Duke of Richmond and by Lord Hay, who bred them. And all Pekinese including my little beauty here, are descended from that royal strain."

Mucketty-hi-ki was sitting haughtily on a brocaded chair beside his mistress.

"Do you tell me," demanded Mrs. McNulty, with serene good humour, "that a dog of such lineage would debase himself to the extent of rummaging in your garbage cans?"

She laughed lightly, as Queen Victoria might have laughed.

"Are you suggesting," she inquired further, "that this little gentleman would associate with such dogs as one finds down the street?"

The little gentleman, one of whose eyes looks east and the other looks west, providing he is facing north or south, and vice-versa, if he is facing west or east, yawned widely, accepted a lick of tea which Mrs. McNulty offered him in a saucer, and then stared blandly, in the Pekinese fashion, not at, but past, the delegation of ladies.

So, in an aroma of tea and Royal Doulton, the visit came to nothing.

And the garbage cans continued to be overthrown, the Harrises' newly-planted tulip bulbs, $14 worth of them, were all dug up, a new postman was chased clean off the street by a posse of nine dogs, with a certain little gentleman ceremoniously bringing up the rear.

It was Thompson, across the street, who came up with our plan of campaign.

68

"He wouldn't deign," said he, "to rummage in our garbage cans, eh?"

So the next morning after my garbage-can lid went clank, there was a community trap set for Mucketty-hi-ki.

"If," we all said, gathered in the dark around Thompson's side drive while the trap was laid, "we can only demonstrate to the old lady that a dog is a dog, regardless of his lineage . . ."

"It's like human beings," said Harris. "There's bad eggs, even in the best of families."

The trap consisted of Thompson's garbage can. On the floor of it was a whole tin of sardines dumped out. We figured sardines would be Mucketty-hi-ki's favourite pollacking. The garbage-can lid was propped up with a light stick, which would fall as soon as the sardines were touched. And there would be Mucketty-hi-ki, trapped IN a garbage can! We all agreed, conspired and confederated together to keep our dogs in, the next morning.

Shortly after 6 A.M., Thompson heard his garbage-can lid go clank. He rushed out in his dressing gown and put his foot on the lid. Inside there was a furious threshing around.

A dozen of us gathered. We telephoned to Mrs. McNulty to come at once and rescue her dog.

"My dog, as you call him," she fluted, "is here in his cot beside me."

Thompson lifted the lid. Inside were both the Lavenders' Siamese, very sticky with sardiney olive oil.

"They must have got out," sobbed Mrs. Lavender, "when the milkman left the milk."

There is always something doing on our street.

69

The Lift Home

ON ACCOUNT of the sleet, I was standing back in the lingerie-shop doorway at the bus stop.

How Pete Wallace saw me I don't know.

"Hey Greg! Want a lift?"

I ducked over to the curb.

"Thanks, Pete," I called gratefully, "but my brother is picking me up."

Of course, my brother wasn't picking me up. He lives miles west in another part of the city. But on such an afternoon, I didn't want any part of a ride in Pete Wallace's car. Why do you suppose I was sneaking off home at 4 P.M.?

I wanted to beat the crowds and the traffic, that's why. When the roads are as slippery and treacherous as this, I like to be safe in a great big fat bus. And the bus drops me within one hundred yards of my front door.

No, thanks. Not Pete Wallace. He's one of these middle-aged drag racers. To him, city traffic is just a sport, to be enjoyed.

I got back into the lingerie-shop doorway along with five or six others; and in a couple of minutes the bus arrived, and I got aboard and found a seat near the back. True, the woman who got the seat behind me took off her hat and shook the sleet down the back of my neck; and the woman in the seat ahead of me threw back her neck fur with a flip and sprayed me all over the face. But as I say, even so, a bus is a good big fat solid vehicle on such a day as this.

I figure we were ten to fifteen minutes longer reaching my block on account of the slowed-up traffic, and the bus was pretty stuffy with the smell of wet cloth. But through the dim window I made out my neighbourhood and got off with little more than the usual squashing. I bent my head and made a run for the house.

As I passed my garage, I was surprised to see the door open and the car gone. (I don't drive my car in this kind of weather.)

When I pushed in the vestibule, a group of my womenfolk rose to meet me.

"Ah, she found you!" they said.

"Who?" I inquired.

"Your wife," said they.

"My wife?" I protested.

"Didn't she pick you up?"

"I came on the bus," I informed them.

"But," cried my womenfolk, advancing on me, "there was a telephone call from your brother that you were expecting HIM to pick you up. And as he couldn't make it, he called and asked if WE could do it."

"My brother?" I checked.

"Yes," they said. "He met a Mr. Wallace in a cigar store up near here, and Mr. Wallace told him you were standing on a corner downtown, in all this sleet, waiting to be picked up by your brother. That's what he told him."

"Well, but . . ." I reasoned.

"But your brother," went on my womenfolk, "had an appointment he couldn't possibly switch. So he asked your wife if SHE would run down for you."

"In all this SLEET!" I gritted. (I not only don't drive my car in this kind of weather. I discourage my wife and all my other womenfolk from taking the car out of the garage.)

"Just before you came in the door," they said, "a Mr. Burt from your office phoned to ask if you were home. And when we said Mrs. Clark had gone down for you, he just hung up."

"Hold it!" I commanded, and headed for the pantry, where the phone is.

I dialled the office.

"Mr. Burt, please," I said.

"He's not in," said the young woman whom I recognized as the new stenographer.

"Has he been gone long?" I inquired.

"He's out with the others," she said, "looking for Mr. Clark."

"But THIS is Mr. Clark!" I informed her sharply.

"Oh, where are you?" asked the girl politely.

"I'm HOME."

"Well, they're all out searching for you," said the girl. "Mrs. Clark phoned from a lingerie shop that you were to meet her at the corner."

"I was NOT!" I stated. "This is all a mix-up. Is there an office boy or anybody you could send out to try and catch Mr. Burt or any of them?"

"No, sir," said the girl. "They're ALL out, boys and everything. Mr. Burt is afraid you were taken ill or something, or had a loss of memory."

"Awffff!" I snorted.

"Asphasia, I think they call it," said the girl. "I would go and look for them, only the telephone . . ."

"No, no," I directed her. "I wouldn't have you go

out in all this sleet. But if anyone calls in, tell them I'm HOME!"

"Yes, sir."

My womenfolk were assembled at the pantry door.

A situation like this calls for decisive action and clear thought.

"I'll take a taxi," I said defiantly.

"Oh, not those!" cried my womenfolk with one voice. "They drive like maniacs."

"I'll take a taxi," I repeated firmly. "Some of the search party are bound to be around that corner, still looking. I can't bear the thought of them wallowing around in all this weather."

I dialled for a taxi.

"Twenty minutes' delay," the despatcher told me. "Twenty minutes to half an hour, due to the weather conditions."

I hung up.

"I'll go back by bus," I announced, rebuttoning my coat with resolution.

"What if anybody calls?" asked my womenfolk.

"Tell them," I said, "to all go home and forget about it."

They ALL phoned while I was downtown riding the bus: my wife, Mr. Burt, three other people from the office, my brother Arthur, and even Pete Wallace.

They all went home. I figure they got there shortly after 5 P.M.

I arrived at the corner and stood in the lingerie-shop doorway. While I was there five buses came and went, in all the sleet.

Then I came home, soaked, arriving at 6:10 P.M.

As for Pete Wallace, you know what HE can do.

Trespass

THREE things will bring me hustling to my window; fire reels; the screech and crunch of a motor collision; and voices raised in angry altercation.

Especially voices raised. I haven't heard a good neighbourly row for years. What's happened to us?

It was to my back window I hustled when I heard the unmistakable voice of Bill Thompson, my old neighbour yelling:

"Oh yeah? Is that SO? Oh yeah! Well, you just try it!"

When I looked out, there was Bill standing at the foot of his small back yard yelling across the low wire fence at both Mr. and Mrs. Cuttlebone, our new neighbours, who were standing in their yard not ten feet from him.

And Bill's three small sons, including Peewee Thompson, the oldest, a great friend of mine, with four or five other neighbour boys, were grouped motionless behind Bill, their hockey sticks in hand.

And in her garden, next to the Cuttlebones, stood old Mrs. Lewis, whom we all call the Peacemaker.

It was quite a tableau, and I knew at a glance what had happened. The puck had gone, once more, into the Cuttlebones' yard, and one of the boys had vaulted the fence to retrieve it. Doubtless Peewee.

"Look!" shouted Mr. Cuttlebone. "This is final. If any of those kids jump that fence once more, I will lay a charge of trespass against YOU!"

"Me?" snorted Bill Thompson.

"I see you don't know the law," cried Cuttlebone. "You are responsible for your children, and also for anybody else who, enjoying the use of your property, commits a trespass on my property. Do you get that?"

"Look," said Bill. "A puck goes over the fence . . ."

It was Cuttlebone's turn to raise his voice.

"Once more!" he shouted. "Once more, and I'll slap an action for trespass on you!"

The Cuttlebones turned their backs and walked into their house.

Bill and the hockey players went into a quiet huddle.

Mrs. Lewis, detecting me at my window, waved me a little twiddle of her fingers, and retired into her house.

The real trouble, of course, is not the puck or even the little boys swarming over fences. It is the yards. There is a natural antipathy between people who keep a back garden as beautiful and trim as the Cuttlebones', and people whose back yard is such a year-round mess as the Thompsons'—full of bare mud, goal posts, forts, igloos in season, footballs, baseballs, bicycles and endless clamour.

Or maybe it isn't the yards. Maybe it is boys. The Cuttlebones are childless. They moved in amongst us a year ago, and have been trying to elevate the neighbourhood ever since.

I watched while Bill Thompson admonished the boys quietly and then went thoughtfully in his back door. The boys resumed their hockey game in a half-hearted

75

sort of way. The goal posts, at either end of the battered dirt yard, were cartons.

My telephone called me from the window.

It was the Peacemaker, Mrs. Lewis.

"I've got a big piece of glass down cellar," she said.

"A what?"

"One of my cellar windows," she explained in a low voice, "was broken by a baseball in September."

"Aw, I know," I said. "I've had a couple of windows bust, but . . ."

"I've broken windows, in my time," said Mrs. Lewis. "I used to be a tomboy when I was little."

"Mrs. Lewis!" I scoffed at the very idea.

"Well," she said, "I've got this big piece of glass down cellar. It was left over when the men repaired the window.

"Yes?" I inquired; for the ways of the peacemaker, as ever, are often hidden from the eyes of men.

"You go back up to your window," she said, "and watch what happens."

"Right-o!" I said enthusiastically. "Right away."

I hurried to my back window.

In about three minutes, Mrs. Lewis appeared at her side door, which is on the mutual drive between her and the Cuttlebones.

In her hand I could see, by the glint, she was carrying a large piece of glass, the corner of which appeared to be broken off. It was, you might say, a large fragment, almost the size of a cellar window pane.

In her other hand, she carried a small iron poker.

She walked to the ash cans which stand a little this way from her side door.

She placed the glass over an ash can.

And with a tomboyish swipe, she shattered the glass into a hundred splinters.

At this dreadful sound, all the little hockey players froze in horror, their faces staring in different directions, their voices stilled.

And in that moment of utter silence, the Cuttlebones' back door bust open and out leaped Cuttlebone, with Mrs. Cuttlebone on his heels.

He raced down the garden, leaped over the little ornamental wire fence, charged the nearest boy, whom he grabbed by the shoulder and, still charging, grabbed Peewee.

And out the Thompson back door bounded Bill Thompson.

"Let go of that boy!" gritted Bill.

"I've got them red-handed!" cried Cuttlebone. "Red-handed!"

Peewee picked up the puck and held it aloft, in mute witness.

"Red-handed what?" demanded Bill Thompson loudly.

"They smashed my window," shouted Cuttlebone. "One of my windows. I warned you! Smashed a window into a thousand . . ."

I slid up my window higher.

"No, no!" I called pleasantly, delighted to be in on the act.

All eyes turned to me.

"No, no!" I repeated in a soothing and most neighbourly voice, full of toleration and goodwill. "It wasn't a window, Mr. Cuttlebone. What you heard was Mrs. Lewis over there, breaking some glass."

77

Mrs. Lewis, poker in hand, came part way down her yard, eyes wide.

"Why," she said, "the ash men won't take a whole big piece of broken glass. They asked me to break it into small pieces to put in the ash can."

She held up the other hand, in which was a corner fragment of the glass she had been holding.

"What," demanded Bill Thompson in a clear, ringing voice, "are you doing in my yard?"

"Well, I . . ." said Cuttlebone, "I heard the crash of glass, and naturally supposed . . ."

"This is trespass, mister!" said Bill. "And, I would add, intent to assault my children."

"Aw, well, now, look . . ." said Cuttlebone.

But under the level stare of Bill, seven little boys, Mrs. Lewis and me, Cuttlebone retreated over the fence and, holding Mrs. Cuttlebone's elbow, vanished in his back door.

Mrs. Lewis winked up at me. I winked at her. She winked at Bill. Bill winked at her. Then Bill and I exchanged a long, slow, appreciative wink.

Blessed are the peacemakers.

Chip-chip-cherry

WHEN I walked down to the Straw Market in Nassau harbour, there were five surreys with the fringe on top waiting for customers in the bright sun of 10 A.M.

I pick my surreys by the horses, not the drivers. This causes considerable disturbance even in the calm serenity of the Bahamas.

You are supposed to take the first one in line.

But a disturbance always seems welcome in Nassau. It breaks the monotony of the Caribbean blueness, the crystal charm. The ladies seated around their displays of straw handicrafts—the purses, bags, hats, mats—struggle to their feet and come smiling eagerly to surround the disputants. It is like a scene from a Strauss operetta, all black but me.

The third horse in line was definitely the best. Its driver, not expecting to be called upon for some time to come, was sagged sound asleep on the cushioned seat of his surrey, in the sweet shade of its fringed top. A very large, jet-black man he was, with the look of a cherub on his sleeping face. It took three pats on the fat thigh to waken him. But it was the immediate tumult raised by the other drivers and the straw-handi-crafter ladies that really roused him.

"Sir," he said, above the protests of his fellow drivers, "you are expected to take the first conveyance in line."

They speak the most beautiful English in Nassau.

"I," I stated with dignity, "am the King of Caractacus, and I always take whatever horse I prefer."

The hubbub dwindled to a murmur.

"You are not REALLY the King of Caractacus?" asked one of the offended drivers cautiously. "Sir?"

"Who," I demanded, gazing sternly around the ring, "is to deny it?"

Obviously, there was nobody. So one of the other drivers reached out and took the bridle of my driver's horse and drew him out of the line.

"Where, sir," asked my driver, coming awaker every moment, "do you wish me to drive you? Would you care to see the late Sir Harry Oakes' mansion and lordly estate? Or . . ."

"No Oakes," I said. "I wish to see birds."

"Did you say birds, sir?"

"I am a bird watcher," I announced, "and I wish to drive very leisurely around the quieter roads of the neighbourhood, amid gardens, amid woods and plantations, with plenty of stops, occasionally getting out to have a better look."

From my straw bag, ornamented with bright flower designs, which I had bought the night before from an old lady on the lawn of my hotel, I drew my binoculars.

"Aaahhhh," said everybody.

"I know, sir," said my driver. "You would like to see the Chip-chip-cherry and hear him sing."

"Exactly," I said, climbing into the back seat of the surrey.

"Then, sir, you love music."

"I do," I said.

"In that case, sir," said the driver, joyously, "you

perhaps would like to have my cousin come with us, with his guitar, and he could sing as we go along."

"Hector! Hector!" called everybody—the other drivers, the straw ladies, turning to face across the market.

Under three palms were several recumbent figures resting with their backs against the boles.

When Hector got up, I could see he had a guitar hung across him.

"This is my cousin, Hector," said my driver. "He will sit in front with me, and amuse you with very good songs, old songs, new songs, whatever you wish."

"Splendid," I said.

"How," asked the driver, turning to face me eagerly, "would you like to have another of my cousins, Henry, to sit beside you while we drive, and he could harmonize . . ."

"Henry! Henry!" cried everybody.

And another figure rose slowly up from the bole of the palm and sauntered across to join the ever-growing congregation.

He too had a guitar.

"This gentleman," explained my driver to him, "wishes to see the birds. I am going to show him the Chip-chip-cherry and many others too. He wishes you to come with Hector and sing."

Henry climbed in beside me in the back seat.

The audience parted and drew back, smiling, looking grave, looking happy, an expression of kindly formality on their shining dark faces.

"This gentleman wishes to see birds," they explained to one another in various tones of surprise and sophistication.

Thus to the old-fashioned sound of a horse's hoofs

and the clatter and rumble of the wheels we went a little way out the pavement and turned up a quiet, unpaved road into the higher land of the island.

Hector and Henry strummed their guitars and sang some do-it-yourself songs for me until we reached a cluster of stately bungalows amid palms and bright flowering garden shrubs; and out of the corner of my eye I saw a flash of black and orange—a Redstart, as sure as you live. And I commanded silence and the surrey jerked to a halt.

"A Butterfly Bird," said Hector.

"Redstart we call it, in my country," I said.

"Caractacus, sir?" asked the driver.

In the shining silence, we heard another small bird singing. A vireo, to my ear, not unlike a Red-eyed Vireo.

"Ah," said Hector, "that is the Cheap-John-Stirrup!"

"No, no," said the driver. "It is called the John-Chew-it."

"I have heard it," said Henry, "called the Sweet John, and also the John Phillip."

Every name they uttered described the song of the little bird to perfection.

I got down and peered up into the palms with my glasses and got the bird, a vireo, bobbing and prying amid the leaves and uttering his busy song, just like a Red-eye. Hector, Henry and the driver all got down and had a look through my glasses.

"Yes," said Hector, "that is Cheap-John-Stirrup, all right."

"John-Chew-it," said the driver firmly.

A white lady in a sun suit came out on the veranda of the bungalow to see what we were looking at.

"It is a small bird," I called, apologetically.

"Ah, yes," said the lady, very English accent, "that is the Cheap-John-Stirrup. It is sometimes called John-Chew-it, locally, or Sweet John. They have local names for everything . . ."

We got back in the surrey in polite silence.

"Of course we have local names, sir," said the driver. "This is a local place. Now I must show you the Chip-chip-cherry. Sktch, sktch!"

Up little hills, down little dales, amid palms, florid bushes, immense grass tufted with silk, past castle-ettes, bungalows, hovels, with guitars now and then, and now and then a song, with many a stop, we saw Pick-Peter or Kingbird; Tom Fool, or Stolid Flycatcher; Bessie-kick-up, a tiny warbler; and the Four o' Clock Bird, which is the mangrove cuckoo. I give you the names Hector and Henry and their cousin, the driver, gave, for preference.

Mary-shake-well, Chick-of-the-Village, Gie-me-a-bit and Killykadick—to you and me, vireos, nighthawks, and other old familiars hidden under names as old as Africa's imagination.

But no Chip-chip-cherry.

"How big a bird is it?" I asked, as we clopped down to the Straw Market at noon.

"Rather large," said Hector.

"Somewhat small," corrected my driver.

"What colour is this Chip-chip-cherry?" I persisted.

"Bluish," said the driver.

"I would say reddish," said Hector. "About the size of a ploward."

So in the Straw Market, with sundry interested witnesses, I paid them two English pounds sterling for a couple of childish hours in the life of an old man.

The Heel

"FOR WHAT do we live," wrote Jane Austen one hundred and fifty years ago, "but to make sport for our neighbours, and laugh at them in our turn?"

Well, I don't mind my neighbours laughing at me. I can laugh right back at them. They're stuck.

It's these blamed transients who irk me—people you'll never see again. And they go snorting on their way entirely misunderstanding the situation.

For example, this girl was walking ahead of me in the downtown noon crowd, and an extremely attractive girl she turned out to be.

Actually, until what happened did happen, I was completely unaware of her. In big cities, it is like that. You can't see the trees for the forest. Walking in the noontime throng you are just a molecule. If, at my age, you want to see a girl, you want to see her at fifteen feet. Or more.

But I was right behind her, my stick hung on my arm so as not to trip anybody with it, and my hands in my overcoat pockets. A decent, comfortable, respectable old citizen with his thoughts far away.

We came to one of those sheds the construction industry builds over the sidewalk where they are doing excavations for new buildings. A sort of covered way.

And we all had to slow up and crowd through in single file.

In the pavement was an iron grille.

The girl's silly shoe caught in the grating.

She lurched forward.

She threw herself backward.

And, protectively, I snatched my hands out of my pockets and caught her as she fell against me.

"Oh, oh, OH!" she cried, turning and clutching me.

It was then that I saw, though she was taller than I, that she was very attractive.

"What is it, dear?" I asked kindly.

"My shoe!" she gasped, hopping up and down, and clinging firmly to me.

Though the crowd was bumping us in the narrow shed-like passageway from both sides, we looked down.

And there, in the muddy grating, was the shoe stuck by its tall, silly heel.

"Hold steady," I said, "and I'll get it."

For she did not want to put her other foot, in its nylon, down on the slushy-tracked pavement. She held it up, and hopped.

"Oh, please!" she cried, clutching me as she staggered.

I honestly believe that those immediately pushing against us perceived the situation, though it was rapidly assuming the proportions of a mob in that narrow passageway.

"Here!" came a strong voice over my shoulder. "You leave her alone, you old — !"

From third back in the crowd a powerful arm came through and grasped my overcoat and gave a yank.

"He's HELPing me!" squealed the young lady, clinging fast to me so as to keep the one foot in the air.

85

But it seems that in the natural din of the traffic and the bunched-up pedestrians in the covered way, all that came through was the word "HELP."

That did it.

From the third and fourth rows back in the blockade, valiant figures crushed forward, both male and female, some tall, some short, some young and some old, some with short umbrellas with which to belabour me and knock my hat off, while they rescued the lovely damsel from my clutches.

"My SHOE! My SHOE!" cried the young lady, as loyal arms supported her from all sides, and as rough elbows and forearms, and a few short umbrellas in ladies' hands, thrust me back, back, from my intended victim.

Every eye was filled with astonishment and horror.

"Imagine!" said one lady. "In broad daylight!"

"Probably," remarked a gentleman of about my own age, "he's nuts."

But after about a minute, though it seems now an hour, I was able to release myself from custody and edge along to retrieve my hat.

And as I stooped for it among the legs, I saw the shoe still stuck fast in the grating. So I retrieved it at the same time, while down.

And by now her rescuers were beginning to understand what the young lady was trying to tell them.

Thus, when, holding the shoe high, I bumped and butted my way through the blockade toward her, there arose a few titters, then a few snickers, then some snorts, and finally:

"Ho, ho, ho! HAW, HAW, HAW!"

The young lady took the shoe and saw, as I had

already seen, that the tall, silly heel had been partly torn loose.

The crowd was dispersing, edging away again in single file in the two directions. Heh, heh, heh! Ho, ho, ho! Hee, hee!

So I, with my stick supporting us in my right hand, and she, holding my left arm most gentlemanly offered, hippety-hopped on one foot and the toe of the other, keeping the twisted heel off the pavement.

And we turned the corner and went along a few doors to where there is a joint shoeshine parlour and a small shoe-repair establishment.

And as we sat, while the Greek, with ancient dignity, nailed the heel back into place, the young lady and I wiped off my hat, the tails of my coat and her nylon, which had, in spite of all, got a little slush on it.

"People," she said, "are AWFUL, aren't they!"

"Hee, hee, hee!" I agreed bitterly. "Ho, ho, ho! HAW, HAW, HAW!"

You see what I mean.

The Shirt

IT was exactly what I wanted. In fact, it was the best-looking shirt I had seen. The back was a beautiful lustrous yellow, and the front was lipstick red. The sleeves, even, were parti-coloured, their fronts red, and the rear halves yellow.

I picked it off the counter and examined it with mounting excitement. Maybe a little large for me, but I could wear it over a sweater. That would pad it out nicely.

This yellow-and-red combination, of course, is the very latest fashion among sportsmen. Red has been considered, for years past, the only safe colour to wear in the bush, hunting. It was long believed to be the accepted garb of the sportsman so that his fellow hunters wouldn't mistake him for a deer and shoot him. But in the past three or four years, as the result of expert research, it has been found that red can be very well mistaken for brown in the woods; whereas yellow is the colour that assures the sportsman of absolute safety.

I looked around for a salesman. I had little time to waste.

All three of them were engaged with customers in other parts of the store.

"Harmphh!" I said, to try to attract attention.

The beauty of this shirt, I realized, as I turned it this way and that in growing appreciation, was that in walking in the bush, the less-visible red side would be toward any game you might approach, while, from the back, the blazing yellow would safeguard you from any trigger-happy sportsman in that direction.

"Is . . . uh . . . ?" I said, loudly, in the hope of catching the eye of one of the salesmen.

But they and their customers all turned their backs impatiently. It was one of these small, jumbled, prosperous little men's-clothing stores you find in these little towns on the fringes of the north country. I would like to have spent an hour in it, groping amidst the piles of shirts, mackinaws, the fine heavy woollen pants you seldom see in the city stores. All kinds of treasures.

But here I was, with the finest shirt I had ever seen, right in my hands, and down the street half a block, at the Chinese restaurant, were the rest of my gang, the four of them, probably right now waiting out beside the car for me. We had seventy miles still to go to the hunting camp, and had just stopped for a quick bite before dark.

And I had gulped my food and told them, as they finished their coffee, that I would only be a jiffy, up the street, to buy a shirt of some kind to replace the one the moths had got.

"Say, I wonder . . ." I sang out clearly.

But nobody even looked at me.

I took off my red hunting cap and pulled the lovely harlequin shirt over my head, parka style. As I had foreseen, it was a trifle large for me. But as I was wearing my black-and-white checked hunting shirt, it wasn't too bad.

I patted it down to shape, put my cap back on and looked about for the mirror that is usually in these men's shops somewhere behind a door or in a dark corner behind a stack of cartons.

There was no sign of it.

Then, I recollected that the glass in the front door of the shop would serve as a sort of mirror, just for a quick check to see it didn't make me look too bulky, or didn't hang down too low.

I went to the door, opened it, closed it and was just in the act of turning around to face the glass when the door was practically jerked from my hands.

And a very large, ugly-looking man took one jump and seized me by the scruff of the shirt.

"No, you DON'T!" he shouted.

Two clerks and a couple of other men swarmed out after him and surrounded me.

"Hey, just a minute!" I croaked, for the collar was tightening around my neck.

They hauled me back into the store.

"Take it off!" shouted the large ugly man, giving me a shake.

He didn't wait for me to take it off. He seized it by the shoulders and practically dropped me out of it.

"Can you beat THAT!" cried the big man. "A little wee squirt like this trying to sneak off with my shirt!"

"There's a lot of queer characters around town at this season," said the storekeeper. They were all ranged between me and the door.

"What do we do with him?" asked the big man, putting the shirt on, himself.

Apparently he had taken it off and laid it on the counter while he was trying on something else.

"May I explain?" I said loudly.

After considerable ho-ho-ing and other derisive sounds, they slacked off to let me be heard.

"I'm with a party," I said, "that's waiting down the street at the Chinaman's. We're on our way up to our hunting camp. I ran out to buy a shirt. And since everybody in the store was busy, I looked around and found this one."

"You might have known," said the big man skeptically, "that was no local shirt. That's an AMERICAN shirt! The latest thing. You don't get THAT kind of thing up here!"

"Since nobody was around to wait on me," I said, "I just hurried and tried it on."

"And sneaked out!" said the big man.

"I was going out," I stated, "to see my reflection in the glass of the door."

"Well, well, WELL!" said the big fellow.

He certainly looked handsome in that shirt. I could have wished a less belligerent man was wearing it.

He glanced around at the group.

"Well," he said, "I'd better get on my way before I lose my shirt."

He strode out.

"I figured," said the storekeeper to the clerks and other customers, "he wasn't going to buy anything. He's the kind that just likes to show off what HE'S got."

"Well, I hope you didn't think I . . ." I said.

"No, no," said the storekeeper. "All the customers use the front door for a mirror."

He patted my shoulder as he accompanied me to the door.

I hustled down the street to the Chinaman's.

The boys were still finishing their coffee.

"Did you get a shirt?" they asked.

"No," I said, "I didn't see anything that fitted me."

The Watch

I NEVER knew or observed an unphilosophic watch-maker. They are a race apart. Very quiet men, detached, infinitely patient, sublimely agreeable. It seems their profession calls for a special temperament. Dealing as they do with instruments of precision, peering through their loupes—that is what those one-eyed mag-nifiers they stick in their eye-sockets are called—at machinery so tiny, so delicate, so perfect to the thous-andth part of an inch, watchmakers appear to develop a set of intellectual standards so different from those of the generality of us that they might be said to be the pioneers of the technological age. Maybe in one hun-dred years, we shall all be as benign as watchmakers.

E. R. Conery has been looking after the Clark watches for two generations of us. His shop is down amid the topless towers of finance. Most of his clients are brokers, bankers, lawyers. There isn't another shop of any kind for blocks around. Conery's is an office, not a shop. And fitly so. For Mr. Conery is actually a watchmaker. To get his degree, he had to construct a watch entire, from start to finish, the gears, the sprockets, the springs, the escarpments, the jewels, the dial, the hands, the case. I didn't know until Mr. Conery told me, after twenty or thirty years of acquaintance, that a watchmaker actually has to have made a watch. By hand. Otherwise, you are something else, but not a watchmaker. I was very interested in this, because as far as I can find out, my great-grandfather was the first native-born watchmaker in Toronto.

Conery's was crowded with seven people when I stepped in off Jordan street—so-called after Jordan Post, the city's first watchmaker, a gentleman from the New England States who blew in about 1795 and presently took my great-grandfather, Thomas McMurray, as an apprentice.

Some of the seven were bringing watches in for repairs, other were waiting to pick up their watches. (Three weeks at the earliest, at this time of year.)

But two of the seven were an elderly lady and her daughter.

They were buying a watch for Christmas.

A dozen watches were laid out on the counter.

"I like this one," said the elderly lady.

"But Mother," protested the younger one, "it's so plain, so severe."

"I can SEE it," said Mother, slipping it on her wrist and holding it up.

It was a very good-looking watch. By no means as small and dinky as others on the counter, it was still a little jewel of grace and simplicity.

"It looks like a watch a nurse would wear," said the daughter, who wore a pink hat and a mink coat. "Or maybe a lieutenant in the CWACs."

"It is a very fine watch," said Mr. Conery. "Incidentally, it is the most expensive watch of the lot."

"Oh!" said Mother, quickly slipping the watch off her wrist.

The daughter immediately changed tactics.

"Why, Mother, if that's the one that appeals to you . . ."

"No, no!" said the older woman hastily. "You're quite right. It is a little severe. Now, let's look at one of these . . ."

And she began picking up the several others, tiny little things, some of fancy shape, some decorated, some long, some square, some round.

"My children," she said, "just want to spend money on me."

The daughter spoke aside to Mr. Conery.

"We want her," she said, "to have a good watch for once in her life."

"Any of these are good," said Mr. Conery.

"How much is this one?" asked the older woman.

"That is $84," said Mr. Conery.

"Mercy!" she exclaimed, setting it down as if it were a hummingbird's egg.

"Please," said the daughter, "you wait on these gentle-men while Mother and I decide."

So Mr. Conery attended to us customers, quietly hand-ing out watches repaired; quietly seating himself at his work desk to examine quickly the innards of watches handed in for repair; and quietly announcing the nature of the defect. He works with easy, smiling precision, no hurry, no waste motion. Like a watch, in fact. I being last, when he turned to me, I winked at him, and he knew I wanted to see the last act of the little drama of buying Mother a watch.

For, in low voices the two women had been arguing over the watches all this time.

"Mother," said the daughter, when Mr. Conery stood in front of them, "has spent her whole life giving, never taking. And we decided it was time she began to indulge in little extravagances. So I have insisted she take that watch she first took a shine to . . ."

"It's far too expensive for anyone of my age," protested the older woman.

But she had weakened.

"A finer watch isn't made," said Mr. Conery.

"It looked extremely smart on you," I put in.

"At least I could see the time on it," said the older woman, cheerfully resigned.

All three began looking for the chosen watch.

They poked and sorted among the dozen watches on the counter.

"I had it in my hand a moment ago," said the daughter.

"It was right here," said the older woman.

Mr. Conery sorted the watches into separate groups.

No plain one, plain as a Greek vase.

"Are you sure you didn't put it back in the show case?" asked the daughter.

"No," said Mr. Conery. "I just returned a moment ago . . ."

The two ladies turned and inspected me. But I was standing well along the counter.

They looked at the floor. Mr. Conery looked on the floor on his side. They all looked behind ash trays, show cards. No trace of it.

"That's the funniest thing!" said the daughter.

"It couldn't vanish," said the mother.

But it had.

"Well, have you another one the same?" asked the daughter.

"I'm sorry, that is the only one in stock," said Mr. Conery. "But I can get you another right away and send it to you . . ."

"No," said the daughter. "We'll be downtown again tomorrow, and we will call in."

"I'll have it here for you," said Mr. Conery with kindly assurance.

The two ladies gathered up their purses and left.

I stared at Mr. Conery in consternation. He looked back at me as calm as a grandfather clock.

"Did they get it?" I husked.

"The elder lady," said Mr. Conery, "has it on her wrist. It got pushed up her forearm as she was trying others on."

"But good heavens, man," I cried, "$139!"

"She'll be back," said Mr. Conery, "as soon as she discovers it."

"Aw, what are you giving us!" I rasped. "We've just seen as cool a bit of flim-flam . . ."

"Wait around a few minutes," said Mr. Conery. "They'll be back."

"But . . ."

"You get to know people in this business," said Mr. Conery, seating himself at his work desk and screwing his loupe in his eye. "If you don't get excited, you don't make mistakes."

I was excited. I sat down on one of the customer chairs.

There was a scuffle at the door.

The two ladies burst in.

"Oh, gracious!" wailed the older woman, holding up the watch. "When I put on my gloves . . . when I pulled up my sleeve . . .!"

The daughter waved her cheque book to calm everybody except Mr. Conery, who was quite calm.

Then she wrote the cheque.

And Mother sat down in the other customer chair to puff beside me.

The Bump

MY WAITRESS had tears in her eyes when she came and handed me the menu and arranged the knives and forks in front of me.

"Hullo?" I said. "What's up?"

She sniffed and dusted off the table to stall for time.

"That woman!" she finally said.

"What woman?"

"That one," said my waitress, "second table back of me. The one facing this way, with the other lady and gentleman."

I picked out the one she meant. A smart, executive-wife type, if you know what I mean. The kind that has doubtless made a great success of her husband.

"What did she do?" I asked the waitress, pretending to discuss the menu.

"She's PERSECUTING me," said my waitress.

"Aw, now!"

I studied the lady two tables away. She had that smooth, assertive, self-assured air of those lady TV announcers who sell freezers and other costly appliances. She had the social-register look.

"Last fall, about October," said my waitress, also pretending that we were discussing the menu, "I spilled the French-dressing jug all over her purse and gloves on the table."

98

"Well, accidents will happen," I pointed out.

"That's what I TOLD her," said my friend. "But ever since, every time she comes here, which is about twice a week, she insists on sitting at my table. She'll go and sit in the lobby, there, until my table is free, and then comes SWEEPING in, to sit at it."

"Well, that could be a compliment," I suggested.

"She needles me," said the waitress. "In a low voice, she just keeps saying, 'Careful, now!' and 'Watch out!' She just keeps smiling up at me. And whenever she has friends with her, she tells them the whole story of the way I spilled the French dressing all over her purse and gloves."

She began to get the sniffs again.

When I glanced over to the second table, the lady was watching me with intent grey eyes and the cool mirth of the born persecutor.

"Aha," I said. "She's caught us talking about her."

Indeed she had. She was now telling her two table mates about it. They turned in their chairs to have a look at the waitress and me.

"I feel," said the waitress "that I'll have to throw up my job."

"Now, now," I said. "Don't be silly. Keep your shirt on. Do you know what psychology is?"

"Oh, I've heard of it," said the waitress, poising her book for my order. She looked pretty forlorn.

"Psychology," I said, "usually looks after persecutors. There ARE people like that. They get PLEASURE out of hurting people, defenceless people."

"What'll you have?" asked the waitress, wearily.

"Smelts," said I. "But what's more, Fate looks after

them, too. Fate never forgives tears of humiliation. Fate remembers tears, and exacts payment for them."

"With French fried?" cut in the waitress.

"And a small mixed salad," I said.

While the waitress was away, the lady and I exchanged several stares. She tried to stare me down, in the loftiest social-register style. But I have grey eyes too, and I can put a kind of cool mirth in them, not to mention a little contempt. She lost the duel.

I was wishing I were Fate. I'd fix her.

But, now, to explain how Fate did fix her, I have to describe the layout. Our restaurant is on the ninth floor of a big department store. The eighth is the main restaurant. The ninth is the balcony. A battery of six elevators comes to its stop at this ninth floor, and all noon long, the elevators quietly discharge those coming up to lunch into a sort of lobby. I sit nearest the lobby, so as to be nearest the smelts. The lady and her companions, the waitress, Fate and I, were all there in full view of the elevators.

I ate my smelts. They were good, as usual. The waitress forgot her tears and went over and attended the last requirements of the second table away, enduring the upward smile of the lady.

The lady was leaving a little earlier than her two friends.

She gathered up her gloves, stood up, bade them good-bye and went around by the cashier's booth and turned to approach the elevators.

An elderly clergyman was just ahead of her.

A tall, bony, lean-necked clergyman in the piety of his late sixties and a large Adam's apple.

The elevator at the far end of the battery of six arrived. Its light flicked on. Flicked off.

The clergyman started to run.

The lady, right behind him, started to run, too, a nice social-register sort of lope.

As she neared the elevator, she turned to wave a pretty little finger twiddle at her friends still seated at their table.

At which instant, the elderly clergyman dropped one of his gloves.

He halted abruptly and stooped over to snatch it up.

And the running lady hit him a bump, full belt, knocking him flying on his face right by the elevator door. His umbrella slammed against the wall. His hat rolled. The elevator girl leaped out to help. The lady, slightly askew, was trying to assist the old parson to his feet.

I, of course, was at once over the plush rope that divides the lobby from the balcony; and right behind me was the waitress.

By the time we two had hold of the clergyman, quite a number of others were assembling. "Madam," I asked firmly. "Why did you knock this old gentleman down?"

She was speechless with rage. But it was not I she was looking at, it was the waitress over my shoulder.

"It was an ACCIDENT!" she gritted, straightening her hat.

"Lady," I said, "I saw you butt right into him."

"I tell you," she half-screamed, "it was an accident, pure and . . ."

"Going down, please!" said the elevator girl, briskly.

"I'm all right, I'm all right," gasped the old gentleman, patting everybody around him.

They got in the elevator and the door slid shut.

"Wow!" said the waitress. "The next time SHE comes in, what a big, fat smile I'll have for HER!"

"I think," I said, as we returned to my smelts, "it will be some time before you see her again. In fact, maybe not so long as you and Fate inhabit this balcony together."

"Mmmmmm?" inquired the waitress.

The Trap

AT LUNCH, Joe Bell seemed preoccupied. We all noticed it.

"What's on your mind, Joe?" I inquired.

"Well, as a matter of fact," said Joe, "I've got a nasty little problem at the office."

"Haven't we all?" remarked Cooper.

"We've got a pilferer on the staff," said Joe.

"A pilferer?" we chorused.

"Somebody is pinching stamps and cash out of my cash box," said Joe. "As you know, I keep the petty-cash box in my desk. Naturally, I keep the drawer locked except when I'm at my desk. So it's somebody right around me."

"Maybe," suggested Herriot, "you're just a little sloppy with your arithmetic."

"Oho, not me!" said Joe. "Not ANYBODY with Dorfus, Bangle & Slatt. Not with old Mr. Slatt around."

We all knew Mr. Slatt, since we often dropped in to see Joe at his office in the importing and wholesale agency of Dorfus, Bangle & Slatt. Messrs. Dorfus and Bangle were dead long ago, driven into their graves, no doubt, by the implacable efficiency of their partner, Mr. Slatt. He had come up in the firm through the accounting end. He was a demon for dollars, quarters, dimes, nickels and pennies.

"Fortunately," said Joe, "it isn't much. Maybe four or five dollars a month. I noticed it first three or four months ago. It seemed to me I was short of stamps in the petty-cash box. Then I noticed, on a couple of other occasions, that dimes and nickels were missing. So I kept a record of every stamp and every nickel. And sure enough, about five bucks or so is missing in dribs and drabs, every month."

"Well, haven't you any suspicions?" asked Herriot. "After all, $5 a month is $60 a year you are docking your salary, and that's the price of a darned good fishing trip."

"Heck, who can I suspect?" cried Joe Bell. "You know them all. There's the three stenographers and the switchboard girls. They've been with us for twenty years or more. There isn't one of them would do a thing like that. Then there's old Peters, the accountant, and the three bookkeepers. Pillars of the church, every one. Hand-picked by old Slatt himself. Members of the same congregation . . ."

"There's a little larceny in us all," I reflected. "Look, why don't you just set a mouse trap on top of your cash box, with a couple of letters laid on top of it. And then the next time your pilferer tries to make a small snatch—WHACKO!—you'll give him or her the fright of their life; and that'll be the end of it."

"I've got a better idea," said Herriot. "I used it last April Fool's Day on my two aunties. You know these magic and trick novelty stores? There's one half-way up the block here. They sell a little gimmick made of a spring and snapper, and it fires a cap like the kids use in their toy pistols. I could rig it on your cash box

104

in five minutes. And, boy oh boy, would it ever expose the guilty party!"

We all went back to Joe Bell's office with him, and on the way, we dropped in at the magic shop and Herriot picked out this snapper. You just set it, like a mouse trap, on the inside edge of a box, and when the lid is lifted, the cap goes off with a resounding bang.

Dorfus, Bangle & Slatt's office is the usual long narrow layout, a large open end for the switchboard and stenographer's desks, then a row of private offices down the hall, Mr. Slatt's being the farthest one in. Joe's, as office manager, is about third this way from Mr. Slatt's.

We all trooped into Joe's office, talking loudly about fishing so as to allay suspicions in case the criminal was observing us. Joe unlocked his desk and handed Herriot the little black cash box.

While Herriot went to work on installing the snapper, the rest of us grouped chattily around the entrance to obstruct the view of any nosy passer-bys.

"O.K.," said Herriot, low, joining us. "Now, Joe, don't YOU forget, and lift that lid. Just do without petty cash for a day or so."

Joe accompanied us along the hall and out to the corridor.

"It's times like this," he murmured, "when I step out to the washroom, or am called to another phone, that the job is done. Somebody just slips in, knowing my desk is open, and nobody looking . . ."

BANG!

The loud crack rang through the office and out the door to us standing in the corridor.

Joe wheeled instantly and raced inside.

At a polite distance, we followed.

The girls in the front office were half raised from their chairs in attitudes of astonishment.

Mr. Peters, the accountant, was just emerging from his own door as Joe raced past.

Joe halted at his office door and stood reared back, his hands lifted in horror.

When we drew up behind Joe, there was a shocking sight.

Old Mr. Slatt, his face flushed purple, his hair on end, was standing unsteadily holding the open cash box in his hands and a small whiff of smoke from the cap was wafting away.

"Mr. SLATT!" choked Joe.

"Wha . . . wha . . . wha . . ." said Mr. Slatt.

He laid the box down on Joe's desk and then sank carefully into Joe's spare chair.

"What was that?" he finally inquired after a deep breath.

"Mr. Slatt," said Joe, brokenly, "I am dreadfully sorry. But I put that gadget in the box because somebody has been pilfering stamps and money."

Mr. Slatt took out his hanky and wiped his brow.

"Bell," he said, "I've been waiting for you to report these shortages in your petty cash."

"Well I . . . uh . . ." said Joe.

"My wife," said Mr. Slatt, "is a good, God-fearing woman, Bell, but she has one weakness. She is always asking me to bring home stamps, and to keep her supplied with nickels and dimes for the parking meters. Well, I'm a busy man, and I can't always remember these things. One day last February, I remembered. I came in to you to get some stamps and small change, and you weren't around at the moment. So I helped myself from the petty-cash box, intending to speak to you."

Mr. Slatt felt able to stand by now. He stood up.

"A couple of weeks later," he said, sternly, "I remembered again, and I realized you hadn't reported the shortage."

"I paid it myself, sir," said Joe, "in the hope of detecting the . . . uh . . ."

"Well, Bell," accused Mr. Slatt, "I've been pinching my wife's stamps and nickels ever since, waiting for you to do your honest duty, and report the shortage."

"It's reported now, sir," said Joe.

"How much do I owe you?" asked Mr. Slatt.

Joe produced a memo from another drawer.

"It's $11.30 in cash," said Joe, "and $8.80 in stamps."

"I'll write you a cheque," said Mr. Slatt, and we made way for him.

He walked stiffly down the hall to his room, and I noticed his hair had settled back in place.

The Creeps

THE MOMENT I stepped out of the elevator, I knew I had made a mistake. But as I turned to nip back in, the elevator door softly slid shut in my face.

It was one of those automatic, do-it-yourself elevators. They give me the creeps. There is something ghostly, soft, silent and menacing about them.

Here I was in a dimly-lit concrete cellar. Instead of pushing the main-floor button when I left the third floor, I must have pushed the "B".

That's what comes of doing business with these back-street merchants. I got a signet ring for my birthday, and I wanted a trout fly engraved on it. In the yellow pages, I looked up engravers, and chose one that had an old-fashioned sound to it. It was located in one of those old buildings down a side street off the main downtown area, and when I arrived at the address, I found I had to help myself in this small, coffin-like elevator up to the third floor. I waited a minute or two in the hope somebody else might come along and give me company for the journey. But the quiet, sleepy old building appeared to be uninhabited.

To my relief, the elevator door whispered open at the third floor and I found the engravers after searching around a few complicated narrow corridors lined with offices, all of which seemed untenanted. Then I sought my way back through the echoing hallways to the elevator, popped nimbly in when it crept open, and pushed for down.

And now I stood, a little startled, in this dimly-lit concrete basement, staring at the dingy metal door that had just slid shut.

In the gloom, I could make out a button in the wall to the left of the door. I pushed it.

Half a minute passed. Overhead a few footsteps came and went. The naked light bulb overhead was dim with dust. I put my thumb on the button and held it there for a good ten seconds.

Nothing happened. I put my ear to the door and listened. No sound at all. Not even the shushing sound these do-it-yourself elevators make.

One more good long push on the button, and then I would walk up the stairs.

The stairs? Why not? Much more pleasant than cooped up in that tin coffin.

From the small concrete passageway in which I stood there were three exits. The stairs would be immediately back of the elevator, wouldn't they?

I tried the first exit. It led into a long grey hall at the far end of which another dusty naked bulb shed a feeble light. The second exit opened into a cavernous unlit room full of crates and cartons, all dusty as though they had been there for years. The third exit was into another passageway, shorter and better lit. I went along it, looking for the stairs.

It ended in a door. I pushed the door open. No stairs. Just another long, concrete tunnel with a light at the far end.

109

"Hullo!" I sang out. "Anybody here?"

No answer.

I retreated to the elevator. I hallooed down both the other exits. My voice echoed.

"Hullo! Where's the stairs out of here?"

I took my walking stick and hammered briskly on the elevator door. No response. I pressed the button long and firmly.

"Well, for Pete's sake!" I said.

I went down the other exit where the light burned at the far end.

There was a door there and I opened it.

As I did so, I clearly heard a sudden brief rush of footsteps and then the sound of somebody bumping into something, like a carton or box.

"Hey, there!" I called out cheerily. "Where's the stairs out of here?"

Not a sound.

"Hello!" I shouted. "Somebody there? How do I get out of here?"

The only sound was my own breathing.

I pushed into the room, another cavern full of high-piled crates.

There was no doubt this time. I heard the unmistakable sound of someone furtively tip-toeing back of the crates at the far end of the room.

"Look here," I called, as friendly as could be, "tell me where the stairway is. The elevator doesn't answer and I . . ."

There was the sound of a door closing softly.

It was with considerable caution that I backed out the door I had just come through. I walked hurriedly back through the passage to the elevator.

110

This time I really banged on the door. And I whooped and yelled with every bang of my stick. I was in the midst of the tattoo when the elevator door calmly slid open.

And there was a young lady wearing glasses, staring at me in astonishment.

"The elevator," she said, "doesn't work from the basement."

"I couldn't," I yammered, "find any stairs."

I nipped in. She pressed the button and in a jiffy I was safe out in the main-floor corridor.

Once there, my true spirit asserted itself.

"Young lady," I declared hotly, "who runs this building? I tell you there's some kind of mystery down there, somebody creeping around . . ."

"Mr. Tottem," she said. "The superintendent. That's his office there on the left."

The door slid closed and she vanished.

I shoved Mr. Tottem's door open. He was a thin, elderly man with a faraway expression.

"What kind of a joint," I demanded, "are you running? I got down in the basement in that infernal elevator and couldn't . . ."

"Ah, yes," said Mr. Tottem. "I've reported it and reported it."

"But what's more," I stated with rising indignation, "there's no stairway. And when I was hunting for some escape from that dungeon, there was somebody down there, SOMEBODY creeping around, who wouldn't ANSWER me!"

"That would be Julius," said Mr. Tottem.

"Julius?"

"Our watchman," said Mr. Tottem.

"I called to him," I said, "I yelled. All I wanted to know was where the stairs are, how you get out of the dang cellar. And not only didn't he answer, he dodged away.

Mr. Tottem held up his hand for silence. He turned to a sort of tin ventilator back of his desk. "Julius!" he shouted down. "Julius!"

After a moment, I could hear a muffled sound coming up the ventilator.

"Was there a gentleman down there a moment ago?" shouted Mr. Tottem.

Again there were booming muffled sounds back up the ventilator.

"Ah," said Mr. Tottem, turning to me. "He mistook you for a bailiff."

"A what?" I queried.

"You know," said Mr. Tottem, "a summons, a writ or whatever it is. Julius is in a little difficulty with the finance companies. They're trying to reclaim his automobile, and he's having a lot of trouble dodging them. He supposed you were one of them trying to catch him here on his job."

"A fine thing!" I declared.

"He says," said Mr. Tottem, "you look exactly like a bailiff's man."

It pays to do business out on the nice, safe, populous main streets.

Ladies-Gents

SO far, I have never blundered into the Ladies by mistake.

This is not to say I have never been IN a Ladies. On the Royal Tour, we had a Press Train that ran thirty minutes ahead of the special train carrying Their Majesties. It was a train of sleeping cars and club cars only, and the car I was in had no lady reporters in it. So we used both ends. Our porter told us we could. And I can remember with what a feeling of daring I pushed open the door at the end of the sleeping car, marked WOMEN, and found therein a bunch of my fellow-scribes busy going blutha-blutha-blutha at their ablutions, and shaving.

As I recollect it, the Ladies on trains is a much more cosy and pretty little room than the men's washroom at the other end. It has more and larger mirrors, little dressing tables and upholstered small chairs. Very chic, compared to the spittoony sort of washroom we Gents are obliged to crowd into, very surly in the morning.

Sometimes, though, I have thought with terror of how a dreamy, faraway guy like me, always thinking of something else, could go sixty-three years through life and never once mistake the doors for Ladies and Gents in restaurants, hotels, clubs, waiting rooms, trains, ships, theatres. It's wonderful, when you come to think of it.

Early in life, I suppose, a horror of making this error is ingrained in us.

In us men, I should say. Because the ladies are far more reckless. Twice in my one small life have the ladies barged right in.

The first occasion, when I was younger and more easily frightened, was a truly terrifying experience. As we all know, both Ladies and Gents have an Inner Sanctum. It has a door that bolts; and very often it is only half a door, leaving at least a foot of space open at the bottom.

On this occasion, I was in the Inner Sanctum, quietly reading the newspaper, when, to my profound consternaation, I heard the outer door open and two ladies come gaily in, chatting. The very first thing they did was to try my door!

The very first thing I did was lift my feet up off the floor and hold them suspended for fear they might show.

And the next thing I did was go through an agonizing moment of self-accusation. Had I, at last, come into the wrong one?

The ladies, gaily chattering, were preparing to out-wait me. Their voices were right beside me. I was involved in a panicked turmoil of doubt and confusion, my mind whirling, my feet held up in space, my whole body turning numb with fright.

Then one of the ladies interrupted her friend's chatter to demand sharply:

"What's that?"

There was a silence.

114

THAT, apparently, was the article of plumbing which marks the fundamental difference between the Ladies and the Gents.

There I hung in space while the ladies held their breaths in a consternation as horrible as mine.

"Good grief!" gasped one of them. "We're in the WRONG ONE!"

And with a wild clatter of heels, they burst the door open and fled; and I lowered my feet to the floor.

To tell the truth, I was glad to get the heck out of there myself, EVEN if I was in the right.

The second occasion was only the day before yesterday. It illustrates the feminine approach to this question much better than the former instance.

It was at one of my favourite restaurants, and I was standing in the men's room, having washed my hands, tidying up my fingernails with my nail file.

The door was flung open with that effect of making an entrance which is characteristic of the ladies.

Especially of these two ladies who burst in upon me. They were of that competent type who are either still business girls, though thirtyish or had been business girls and married promising young executives.

Nothing fazes them.

The leading one was the kind who raises one eyebrow very lofty when asking a question.

"What," she demanded, "are YOU doing in here?"

To my great surprise and satisfaction, I did not panic. I did not even run.

"Get OUT!" said the one behind her, in battleship grey, and very smart.

She indicated the door with a long, slim red-tipped finger.

I stood my ground with magnificent aplomb.

I was not dismayed.

With my nail file, I pointed rather elegantly, and in complete silence, to that article of plumbing which, as I mentioned before, differentiates the Gents from the Ladies.

They turned their stylish heads and glanced at it.

"Ow!" screeched the battleship-grey one.

"Yow!" yelled the other, lowering her eyebrow instantly. And the two of them, crouching down in their horror, pushed and pawed at each other as they scrambled madly out the door.

As luck would have it, two gentlemen were just entering, and the ladies had to bump and bustle their way past the men who, slightly aghast, pressed back against the wall to let them by.

One of the newcomers was a clergyman, with his white collar. His companion, middle-aged, looked like his People's Warden.

"Well, well," said the clergyman, deeply, "WELL!"

"Indeed?" said the layman.

They inspected me narrowly in the long mirror, as they bent to the basin.

I finished tidying my nails, put my nail file back in my waistcoat pocket and walked with all dignity out the door.

But here it is: the trouble with having my picture at the top of these stories is that I am easily identified; many people know me whom I don't know from Adam. Or Eve.

So I have just put down these particulars so that no rumours or misunderstandings might get afloat.

All I say is, so far, I have never blundered into any Ladies.

Red Hawk

THOUGH I am largely Scottish myself by descent, with only a little Irish and Scandinavian mixed in, it is with the Scots I have had most trouble. For instance, John Herries McCulloch, a Scottish journalist, author and litterateur, who for several years worked as a newspaperman in Canada, would not believe a word I said.

We were good friends—lunched together, worked on stories together, visited one another's homes. But John had decided from the outset of our acquaintance that I was what he called an imaginary man. John had those agate brown eyes you see in Pictish Scots, and he looked at me with stony unbelief, whether I was telling him how, as a boy, I used to collect live rattlesnakes in potato bags to give to biologists, or regaling him with some fantastic experience I had had in war.

It could be that the whole Scots have an inherent doubt of the partly Scottish.

The more John doubted me, the harder I tried to test his credulity. Indeed, in the second year of our friendship, I must confess I was stretching things a bit. Some of my war reminiscences, for example, became so exciting that they even scared me. Many a tale recounting the exploits of my Canadian pioneer ancestors grew so embellished, so realistic and so sensational that I find difficulty today talking to my grandchildren, sorting from the facts those glorious adventures of my mythical great-grandfathers lest they become part of the

117

family lore of the Clarks. For after all, I am a very honest man, as God knows, if hardly anybody else does.

Amongst the honest facts is this: that one of my great-uncles, an Anglican clergyman, married a beautiful young lady at Sault Ste. Marie who was part Ojibway.

Surely you will agree that this entitled me, as a boy of twelve, fifteen, sixteen, to hold the view that Ojibways were kinfolk of mine. And in that belief, I went out of my way to meet Ojibways, cultivate them, and inform them of my claim to kinship through my distant and long dead great-uncle. It went over big with Indian boys of my own age. The older Ojibways were not impressed.

Among the boys who thus became my friends was Henry Jackson, known in his own tongue as Red Hawk, sometime chief of the Christian Island reservation.

As the years progressed and Red Hawk and I became men, he never came to the city without visiting me at my home or at the office. We would have lunch and enjoy the pleasures of the metropolis while talking about the wilderness. We formed the habit of exchanging a few sentences in Ojibway that Red Hawk had taught me—some of them perhaps not very polite—in order to impress people at neighbouring tables whom we detected listening in. Red Hawk was a handsome man; he dressed finely like a prosperous business man; but he was the true dark rich copper colour of the Redman without any touch of foreign blood in him. It was fun to lunch with him in a smart restaurant and excite the curiosity of the natives.

John Herries McCulloch was walking up the corridor from his office at the far end to the news room at the other end of the building. My office was midway down the hall, facing the elevators.

118

He was in his shirt sleeves. But even in shirt sleeves, John was encompassed with dignity. And he respected dignity in others when he saw it.

And just as he was passing the elevators, one of them opened to discharge a figure of great dignity and even greater impressiveness. It was Red Hawk, dressed in fine worsted, his black hair long, like an artist's or a musician's, his slow gaze sweeping the busy newspaper corridor.

John Herries McCulloch halted instantly.

"Sir," he said, "may I direct you?"

Red Hawk brushed John with his dark, inscrutable gaze. He knew perfectly well where my office was, and required no direction.

But there was something in the courtesy, the Old World dignity of McCulloch that stirred a responsive fibre in him.

"I am Chief Red Hawk," he announced in his deep slow voice. "May I ask your name, sir?"

"McCulloch," replied John. "John Herries Mc-Culloch."

Red Hawk held forth his hand, and the Pict from Galloway and the Ojibway from up around Penetang gravely shook hands.

"Sir, I presume," said John, "you wish to see the city editor?"

Red Hawk drew himself up.

"No, sir, I do not," he answered. "I wish to see my kinsman.

"Your kinsman?"

"My kinsman, Gregory Clark, who is known to my people as Shongwesh."

I was sitting at my desk when I saw the door open slow and wide, and there stood McCulloch in his shirt sleeves, and curiously pale. His agate eyes were regarding me with an extraordinary expression.

Behind him stood Red Hawk, the figure of a chief, erect, his eyes glinting with some sort of mischief.

"*Bojo, Nitchie!*" cried Red Hawk.

By sheer luck, I caught the cue.

"*Coween nishishin Shagenosh!*" I shouted, leaping to my feet and rushing to embrace Red Hawk, who was uttering Ojibway expressions of brotherly affection.

McCulloch was standing with his back to my open door, a look of profound astonishment all over his face, reluctant to move.

"John," I exclaimed, "may I introduce you?"

"We have met," cut in Red Hawk grandly, as if dismissing the stranger. "He has brought me to my kinsman."

When John shut the door, I went into a dance, a war dance, explaining in gleeful whispers to Red Hawk, whom of course I always called Henry, what a ten-strike this was for me.

For from that moment forward, John Herries McCulloch believed everything I told him, regarded my every utterance with the greatest deference, and went back to Scotland in due time respecting me, as he does still in our occasional letters, as a man of tested and undoubted integrity.

A couple of things I never did tell John.

"*Coween nishishin Shagenosh,*" my cry of welcome to Red Hawk, and one of the two or three paltry phrases of Ojibway I know, means "No-good White Man!"

And *Shongwesh*, the name by which Red Hawk said I was known unto his people, means The Mink.

The Pest

"PARDON ME," said the pleasant female voice over my shoulder, "but that's mine!"

"What's the difference?" I inquired.

"My purse is in it," said the young lady.

I had come through the turnstile on entering the supermarket, saw two or three of those wire-basket wagons standing handy, and started off with the handiest one.

In horror, I glanced forward into the basket. There, almost invisible because of its silvery colour amidst the wire, was the lady's purse.

"I BEG your pardon," I said most affably, to show the pretty young lady that I was, after all, a nice respectable elderly gentleman.

"It's all right," smiled the young lady.

But there was a slight expression of suspicion on her bright intelligent face.

She shoved off.

I selected another wagon; and after examining it carefully to make certain there was nothing whatever in it, I shoved off in another direction.

Actually, I am not much of a supermarket customer. We're old enough, in our family, to know pretty well what we want. So we just deal with the good old family grocer, a couple of blocks over on the shopping street.

We telephone for what we need, and they deliver. We don't see the store from one month's end to the next.

But every now and then, just for the heck of it, I like to go on a shopping binge in a supermarket. It is the duty, I always say, of a newspaperman to see what the people are doing. So my wife lets me get loose. In fact, right now, she was sitting in the car out in the parking area, listening to the car radio. It unnerves her to see me shopping in a supermarket.

First I head for the Polish sausage. Polish sausage does not appeal to anybody else in my family. They don't like garlic, for one thing. And, as they say, if they want to chew mukluks, they will go up and join the Eskimos. But I'm rather fond of chewy, old, dry meat. It reminds me of my army days.

So I got a couple of good Polish sausages—a short, fat one, and a long, skinny, wrinkled one. Variety, that's my motto.

Next, fruit juice. The fruit juice is in the second aisle over. And as I briskly rounded the corner, my wagon collided, crash, with the wagon of a lady coming in the opposite direction.

You're right. It was the wagon of the pretty young lady.

"Well," she said

"I AM sorry!" I exclaimed. "It's a small world, isn't it?"

"Very," said she, and swept by.

I got some pawpaw juice, said to renew your youth; a couple of tins of apricot nectar and three or four different brands of tomato juice. Variety, that's me.

Next, pickled eggs.

They were high up on a shelf. Pickled eggs are popular, it seems, with taller people. I had quite a time reaching them. When I got them down, two jars, and backed up toward my wagon, I felt something give.

There was a shocking clatter.

I had backed into a passing customer who, in attempting to take evasive action, had shoved her wagon up against a tall pyramid of canned cherries, a special of the supermarket for the day. So they had erected a pyramid of them to attract customer attention.

Cans were tumbling and rolling in all directions and customers were tap-dancing to escape them when I looked up right into the face of the SAME young lady. It was she who had bumped into the pyramid.

"Well, WELL!" I said, in a tone of the sincerest sympathy.

But she didn't answer, and was flushed up high on her cheek bones, which I am told is the way girls with that bright brown hair get mad.

However, she and I were busy picking up tins when one of the store clerks in a white apron came hurrying, and took over the job of rebuilding the pyramid.

"Well, uh, it seems . . . uh . . ." I said to the young lady.

But she just walked off in one direction. And I took the other.

For the rest of my binge, I was careful to keep my eyes open so as not to run into her again. I carefully scanned each aisle before entering it, to make sure she wasn't in it.

Thus, I got my four loaves of assorted non-Canadian bread, my three pounds of Spanish onions, my two avocados, my bottle of terwhillicken vinegar, or whatever you call it; and a few other stomach-astonishing things, until my wagon was nicely full. And then I headed for the line-ups.

I picked the one with only four people in it.

But, as usual, I had got behind four ladies who operate boarding houses.

It was quite a while before my turn arrived. The line-ups not only behind me, but those at the other two cashiers, were long and weary.

It was in glancing back at these lines that I made the astonishing discovery.

The customer directly behind me was the young lady!

Her face was averted when I glanced at her.

I looked at her wagon. It contained only a handful of items—some oranges, a packet of bacon, a few small tins . . .

Here was my chance to make amends.

"Aw, MY dear young lady," I said, just as I was lifting the first of my purchases on to the counter by the cashier. "Here! Get in ahead of me. You have only a few . . ."

"No, no," she said. "Don't bother."

"Aw, come ON!" I pressed. "I'll be all day."

She quickly scooped up her purchases and I let her edge past me.

But as she stood before the cashier, who was a man in a white apron, he said:

"Sorry! I've already rung up these."

Indicating the things I had set up.

"I'm letting the young lady go ahead," I informed him.

"I can't ball up my cash register," said the cashier,

124

stonily. "Pass around the end, lady, and get in line again."

"But, good heavens, she was next behind . . ." I protested.

"Don't block the line!" commanded the cashier loudly.

The young lady went past, slammed her parcels down on the far end of the counter, and, with shoulders squared and swinging with indignation, marched for the OUT door.

It snapped open, with its electric eye, hardly in time to let her through.

When I, a few moments later, with my two shopping bags full, went through the same door, I glanced apprehensively around the parking area. But there was no sign of her. She'd gone.

"What kept you?" asked my wife when I reached the car.

"Oh, nothing," I said, airily.

The Handyman

"HAVE YOU," asked my cottage neighbour, Sully Sullivan, "got one of those square-headed screw drivers?"

He had walked along the beach from his cottage, the third west of ours, and I had watched him approach from my front steps. He had kicked the sand all the way. Kicked it in obvious irritation.

"Come on in," I said, "and we'll have a look. I think there's one around."

It isn't easy to find things on these early-season week-end trips to the cottage. You are just up to look the place over and see if the roof was caved in by the snow or anything.

Sully followed me into the dark pantry sort of place where everything was shoved out of the way last fall when we closed up.

"These darn' kids!" said Sully.

Sully has four daughters, ranging from about eleven to sixteen.

"Have they bust something?" I inquired, groping around for the egg crate I keep my tools in.

"It's the blooming record player," said Sully. "We've got one of those hand-wind-up record players . . ."

Ah, well I know it. It plays all summer long, morning, noon, night.

126

"Well, it's stuck," said Sully. "And of course you'd think we only came up this weekend in order to play that damn' record player!"

"Girls will be girls," I mentioned.

"Yah! They brought up a whole slew of new records," said Sully. "And they've been sulking around ever since we got here last night. Here I am with a whole raft of jobs to attend to, take off the shutters, repair one window, set up the water pump. And all they do is yammer, yammer . . ."

"Ah," I cut in, hauling forth the egg crate from under all the boat cushions and stuff.

In a minute, we had the square-headed screw driver.

Sully took it out into the living room and studied it doubtfully.

"Is this the only one you have?" he asked.

"Yes, and I don't know how I got it."

"Well, I think it's the wrong size," said Sully. "That's modern industry for you. They invent a new kind of square-headed screw for their own convenience in squashing screws in with an electric machine. And then the parent company invests in a subsidiary company to manufacture three or four different sizes of screw drivers . . ."

"Sully, old boy," I said, "you shouldn't get all worked up like this on your first visit to the cottage. Why don't you do what I do? Just take some boat cushions out and sit on the steps. And don't do a thing!"

"I've got to try to fix that record player," said Sully, "or go nuts."

"Aw, chase them out on to the beach," I advised.

"How many daughters have you got?" demanded Sully. "Daughters are far worse than sons. When sons sulk, they just go away some place and sulk. But daughters have got to sulk out loud. You've no idea . . ."

"Come on," I said. "I'll come along and help you fix the machine and get it over with."

We walked back to Sully's, and he kicked sand all the way.

Two of the girls were sitting on the front steps, their chins cupped in their hands, glowering at the earth.

From the back, the kitchen, we could hear the two older ones arguing in high voices with their mother.

"Women!" said Sully grimly.

The record player, with a handle on one side, was sitting on the table. Records still in their cardboard envelopes were scattered around it.

I gave the handle a tug.

"It's wound solid," said Sully.

We explored and found the screws that secured the upper panel with the turntable to the lower structure of the box.

They were square-holed screws, small, snug and embedded deeply in the wood. One dab with my screw driver revealed at once that it would not fit.

Sully took the screw driver.

"Girls!" he shouted. "Come here!"

From the front steps the two younger ones came with lagging legs, and the older ones, looking daggers, came reluctantly from the kitchen.

"Come here!" commanded Sully. "Now look! You can't fit this screw driver into those holes! Can you?"

The four heads bent down.

"Why," asked the oldest girl, "don't we have an ELECTRIC player like everybody else?"

"Awfffff!" yelled Sully, stamping out on to the verandah.

"Personally, Sully," I said when I joined him, "I wouldn't fool with the machine anyway. Even if you COULD get it open, it would be a lot of involved springs and stuff."

"Thank the Lord," said Sully, "we're leaving for home at 6 P.M."

I took my square-headed screw driver, patted him on the back, and went to my cottage to sit on the boat cushion on the front steps. That's the best part of a pre-season visit to the cottage.

I was still sitting there when I saw Sully and his family drive away from the back of their place about five-thirty. Ahead of time.

We left around seven.

And about thirty miles south on the highway, after you turn in from our gravel road, I was shocked to see Mrs. Sullivan and all four of the girls sitting up on the slope of the road bank, and Sully's car halfway into the ditch, its stern up in the air.

I pulled out of the traffic and walked back. Sully was nowhere to be seen.

"What happened? Where's Sully?" I asked.

"He's been gone an hour," said Mrs. Sullivan. "He hitched a lift to go and get a tow truck."

"It was a mouse," said the oldest girl.

And then they all started talking. It seems they were sailing along at sixty when all three girls in the back seat suddenly saw a mouse scrambling up the upholstery right in front of them. And they let out a scream of such harmonious violence that Sully lost control of the car, swerved off the shoulder and, after a heroic struggle, got it stopped half-way into the ditch.

I was still hearing the lurid details when a tow truck arrived with Sully sitting beside the driver.

"What a weekend!" groaned Sully, as I handed him down from the cab.

The tow-truck man suggested we unload the car to facilitate hauling it out of the ditch.

Along with the suitcases, provision hamper and some curtains Mrs. Sullivan was bringing home to launder there was the record player.

Sully gave it a kick after he placed it on the sod.

I waited to see their engine working, and then left them.

Monday noon, Sully phoned me.

"Hi," he said. "Do you know what was the matter with that record player?"

"Rusted?" I guessed.

"No, there was a mouse nest in it," said Sully. "Packed tight, with five young pink mice in it. That was probably the mother that nearly wrecked us."

"Well, well," said I.

"So I turned the darn' thing in," said Sully, "for an electric one."

When the ladies get together, they sure have their way.

The Match

EVEN a justice of the Supreme Court of Canada, tootling along the highway at only a little more than the legal speed limit, is likely to experience that guilty start we all feel on seeing a police car all of a sudden.

I don't blame the man two cars ahead of me who, on seeing a black-and-white police car coming in the opposite direction, suddenly braked from sixty-five to fifty-five.

I blame the fellow next ahead of me. He was a tail-gater. He was right on the tail of the humble citizen leading our procession. And before he could check, he had slammed into the rear of the humble citizen.

There was the usual kafuffle. Fortunately, I was far enough behind to escape hitting the tail-gater. But we all pulled over to the shoulder.

The policeman, on hearing the racket, had run off on his shoulder, and walked back to us, hitching up his belt in the approved manner.

We all bailed out. The tail-gater was a big, loud-spoken man about two hundred and thirty pounds, with a cigar butt in his teeth. He was followed out of his car by his wife, a very small woman of about one hundred and two pounds.

"How many times," she cried angrily, as we all assembled around the rear end of the car that had been clunked from behind, "how MANY times do I have to tell you not to drive right on the tail of the car ahead?"

She was speaking to her large husband.

"Ssssh, Mary!" he said in a low voice.

Then in a loud voice he shouted:

"What's the idea of slamming on your brakes without any warning?"

The man who had been clunked was a modest little fellow, stoop-shouldered and flustered.

"I . . . I . . ." he explained.

The policeman, tilting back his helmet in the approved fashion, joined us, signalling passing traffic to go on, and then asked:

"Well, well, well! What goes on?"

"Awfffff!" said the small wife of the large offender. "I've been telling him for thirty years NOT to drive right on the TAIL . . ."

"Sssshhh, Mary!" said her husband, out of the other side of his mouth from the cigar.

Then, squaring himself up very large, he declared in a loud voice:

"This here man suddenly slams on his brakes!"

The stoop-shouldered little man fluttered.

"When I saw you, Constable," he said, "so all of a sudden, there, I just slowed a little, to look at my speedometer."

"Ah," said the constable, taking out his book. "I'll just make a note. There doesn't seem to be any major damage. Your driving licences, please."

"He just SLAMMED on his brakes!" shouted the large man.

"How many times," cried his small wife, "have I

TOLD you it was dangerous to drive right up against the car ahead?"

"Mary!" said he, abjectly.

And, looking a little wilted, he groped out his driver's licence.

My wife and I got back in our car, not being needed, and drove on. Being landscape watchers, we were soon passed by the car of the large man and his little wife.

"Ah," I said, noting him. "He's back in command. He's got a new cigar. Look at the way he glares ahead, like the headlight of a locomotive."

Noon caught us in a pretty little town, and we drew into an attractive restaurant for lunch.

Who should be sitting in the booth directly across from us but our large friend and his little wife.

They had almost finished their lunch. She was toying with a large pink sundae. He was glaring.

"I guess," he shouted up the aisle, past a dozen customers, "this is your cook's day off, eh?"

"Noooo," said the proprietor at the cash register.

"You don't mean to tell me," boomed the big fellow, "that this is the food you regularly serve?"

There was silence all over the restaurant.

"Hey, there!" commanded the big fellow. "If you get me a fly swatter, I'll help you clean up the flies."

The small wife bent lower over her sundae, apparently muttering into it.

"Haw, haw, haw!" laughed the big man.

He struggled sideways out of the bench in the booth.

"Take your time, Mary," he commanded. "I'll get a cigar."

Expanding himself, he strolled up the aisle, glancing into each booth as he went. Nobody looked up at him.

133

"What cigars have you got?" he said, loud enough to be heard across the street.

The proprietor took out three assorted packets from the showcase.

"Yah!" said the big man. "Haven't you got anything better than that? No twenty-five centers?"

The proprietor was dumb.

The big fellow selected one package and tossed the coins on the counter in such a way as to make as much noise as possible.

Coming back down the aisle, he addressed himself to the multitude.

"Some joint!" he said. "Not even a decent cigar!"

He squeezed back into the booth.

With large gestures, he undid the packet of cigars and drew one out. He sniffed it loudly, and held it off while he inspected it contemptuously.

"Junk!" he said.

He bit the end off and phutted it into the aisle.

He clamped the cigar in his teeth, tilted up at forty-five degrees.

From his shirt pocket he drew a wooden match and scratched it on the underside of the table.

It broke.

He picked another match from his pocket, scratched it under the table, and lit up.

Smoke, faint and wispy, drifted up around the table, out into the aisle.

"Ouch!" squeaked his small wife, leaping up and dancing out into the aisle.

She bent and batted furiously at her nylons.

"How many times," she cried in a chilling voice,

"have I told you NEVER to scratch a match under a table?"

"Mary!" pleaded the big man, trying to get up.

A waiter came and tossed glasses of water under their table. The broken match had lighted, obviously, and set fire to the small litter of gum wrappers, paper napkins and other by-products of the restaurant business.

"You could have burned the place DOWN!" cried Mary.

When they went to the cash register to pay their check, the big fellow was wilted again.

As the door closed after them, we could hear her voice:

"How MANY times have I . . .?"

The Tickle

ITCHY NOSE? You're going to kiss a fool. At least, that's the old saying. Like an itchy palm: if your palm itches, you are going to receive money.

Now, I've had a tickle on the end of my nose ever since I was about twenty-four. Back in that old Mud War, 1914-1918, a shell went off close enough to throw me several yards through the air; but the only injury was a lot of fine metal dust that peppered my face. I had to cut my moustache off, and it was a dandy. I also got what are called craters in my right eyeball. To this day, I sometimes hit a speck of metal with my razor when I am shaving. Imagine: forty years after.

But it seems I got one on the end of my nose. And every once in a while, I get this tickle on the tip; and I have to take my right index finger and give the end of my nose a brisk little wobble. Most of my family and friends are long familiar with this habit. Many people have little mannerisms of this kind. Nobody minds, I hope. Just a swift little squash and twiddle to the end of my nose. That relieves the tickle.

Well, sir, about a year ago now, I was sitting at the back end of the bus where the seats face each other.

I was minding my own business, as usual, which, being a newspaperman, is looking alertly around at everybody and being aware of all my fellow passengers

That comes as natural to a newspaperman as looking at people's haircuts is to a barber, or as speculating on the health of people comes to a doctor when he sits in a bus gazing at his fellow passengers. A newspaperman is like a spectator at a play, a never-ending play. He sees drama in every man, woman, child. It is wonderful to be a newspaperman.

Well, anyway, there I was spying about me when I got this sudden tickle on the end of my nose.

Unconsciously, I put my index finger on the tip, and gave it the familiar little twiddle and squash. Unconsciously, mind you. I've been doing it for forty years. It is second nature.

And I was in the midst of this small exercise when my eyes caught those of the man sitting directly facing me in the back of the bus.

Never have I seen such a glare as he was giving me.

And I realized instantly that he had the largest reddest nose I have ever seen. It was like the nose of Cyrano de Bergerac as played by Jose Ferrer. It was a banana. No it was a parsnip. It was a great big bold nose such as the Duke of Wellington is said to have had, or those noble Romans who conquered the whole known world and held it against all us short noses for hundreds of years.

There was I, wobbling the end of my nose at him.

And there was he, glaring malignantly.

I snatched my hand away and smiled deprecatingly.

Furious, he cast a swift glance up and around at our fellow passengers.

None was looking. I wouldn't have looked either if I had seen him first.

In fact, I didn't look at him again. But I could tell that he was sitting there, staring at me.

So I did what you would have done in the same dilemma. I turned and glanced thoughtfully out the window, pretended this was where I got off. And I got off.

And took the next bus.

How often in your travels have you had some small embarrassing encounter with a stranger you never noticed before, and thereafter saw him or her every time you turned around?

My friend, large of nose, was on the bus next morning as I was going to the office. I saw him, he saw me, the minute I got on. I went into the public library three days later. There he was, leaning on the desk talking to the librarian. I got out before he saw me. Ten days later, at lunch, I felt somebody staring at my back. I glanced around. There he was, two tables away.

I became conscious of my tickle. Every time I felt my right hand, index finger extended, about to rise and administer the old familiar twiddle and squash to the tip of my nose, I halted it half way, and glanced fearfully around. It became a mild neurosis with me. I got into the habit of letting it tickle. I tried twitching my nose, squirming it around to relieve the tickle, until my family started to protest at the faces I was making.

I guess I have seen my Cyrano thirty times in the past year. If I saw him first, I was able to duck. But every time I failed to see him first, I got from him a glower that indicated he had not forgotten what he deemed to be my rude behaviour in a public bus.

Last Thursday afternoon, much to my delight, I got a long-distance call from Chicago, from my old friend

Pete Waring, that he had got hold of a dozen larding needles in a run-down little old junk shop down near the packing-house region of Chicago, and he had shipped the lot to a dealer here in town. And if I still wanted a couple, I should get in touch with him.

Larding needles? Well, they are an old-fashioned implement butchers used to use, back in my childhood, to lard dry meat such as venison and veal and certain cuts of beef. It is a long, curved needle with a big eye. And you take long, thin strips of fat pork, thread them into the eye of the needle, and then draw them through the meat, dozens of them, so that the fat permeates the whole roast, rendering it juicy and rich. A well-larded roast of venison, before it goes into the oven, is prettily stippled all over with the little protruding ends of the threads of fat.

Pete Waring gave me the name and address of the firm, importers of needles, fancy goods, smallwares, and I phoned them immediately and reserved two larding needles for when they arrived.

This morning, I got the call.

This is something I have been looking forward to for forty years.

It was down in the wholesale district. There was no elevator. So I walked up three flights.

I found the firm's name painted on a glass door.

I entered.

As in most importers', nobody was in sight.

I could hear people about in the region behind the partitions.

I coughed.

It so happened, I got a tickle on the end of my nose.

I gave it the twiddle and squash.

At which very moment, my friend with the parsnip nose appeared around the partition.

I think we were equally paralyzed.

I was so transfixed, I just stood there with the end of my right index finger pressed against the tip of my nose.

He just glared.

I finally felt my blood start to move in my veins again, so I dropped my hand, wheeled, yanked the door open and ran.

All three flights I ran.

Some things you just can't explain.

Tit for Tat

MRS. MUTCH is a dear little old widow whose back yard abuts on mine with only the little wire fence between; and though we have never been in each other's house, we have had countless neighbourly interchanges across the fence. And more than conversation, at that. Plenty of groceries have passed over the fence: a loaf of bread, a bottle of milk, half a pound of butter—whatever either of us has run short of, unexpectedly. We are, as you can see, the kind of neighbours everybody ought to have.

I suppose the reason it has never come to us visiting her house or Mrs. Mutch coming around the block to drop in on us is that she is not the visiting kind. Her husband has been gone so long that she tells me sometimes she forgets what he looked like, and has to run into the parlour, which is the downstairs front room of her house, to look at his picture there on the mantel.

She never had any children, and most of her relatives are dead or in California; so she has retreated, I suppose, into a quiet little world of her own, consisting of her house, her garden and her church. She is a church-going little lady, but doesn't let it get the best of her. I seldom see visitors at Mrs. Mutch's.

She was raking the leaves along the wire fence the other day when I came out in my yard.

"Hi!" said I, walking down.

"Well!" said Mrs. Mutch, resting on the rake. "Did you hear the racket last night?"

"I didn't notice," I confessed.

"Awful!" said Mrs. Mutch, giving the earth a good jag with the rake. "It started about eleven o'clock. I had just turned off the radio. And then it began. First, two or three cars arrived at the house on the south side of me. Then about five cars piled up at the house to the north of me."

"Aw, the kids!" I said.

For Mrs. Mutch is hemmed in on both sides by houses full of teenagers. Elderly teenagers. They're the worst kind—too young to keep quiet, too old to be quelled by their parents.

"Well!" said Mrs. Mutch, giving the earth another fierce jag with the rake teeth. "You never heard such a din. I can't understand why you didn't hear it. By midnight, on both sides, they were howling, hooting, thumping, banging, yelling. TV going, radio going, record players going. All windows and doors wide open. Chasing each other around the yards. Dashing away in cars without mufflers, only to return in five minutes with another load of pop and hot dogs."

"Tsk, tsk, tsk!" said I; for all my teenagers are now grown up and gone far away.

"You'd think," said Mrs. Mutch, "they'd have some consideration for me. I banged my windows shut. I opened them and banged them shut time after time, as a hint. By two o'clock in the morning, I was nearly crazy."

"I suppose," I said, "you didn't consider telephoning the police?"

142

"Oh, you couldn't do THAT!" protested Mrs. **Mutch.** "Not in a nice district like this."

"Don't they ever keep quiet?" I inquired cautiously.

"Well, naturally," said Mrs. Mutch, "they're not very lively in the mornings. They sleep in till the last minute."

Mrs. Mutch looked at me with a sudden expression of inspiration unusual in a person of her age.

"Have you a radio?" she asked, flushed. "One you could spare me for a day or two?"

I went and got the one I keep at my bedside for getting the early-morning newscasts.

"I'll put mine," said Mrs. Mutch, as I handed it over the fence, "at my bedroom window that faces north on three of their bedrooms. And I'll put yours in the open bathroom window that faces south on to two of their bedrooms."

"Be sure," I suggested, "to get the same programme on both radios, or it might look too fishy."

"There are some DREADFUL programmes in the early morning!" said Mrs. Mutch, her hair falling over her eyes in excitement. "Hillbilly tunes, cowboys, quartets all singing through their noses . . ."

"And hootin' and hollerin'," said I.

"Five A.M.," said Mrs. Mutch.

"Rock and roll over," I said.

That night, all was quiet over the fence. At 11 P.M. when I let the dog out for a run in the yard, Mrs. Mutch came to her lighted back door and walked down to met me.

"I'll wait until they stage another party," said she.

"It'll be Friday," I suggested, "so they can sleep in late next morning.

"Ssshhh," said Mrs. Mutch.

Friday night, there was a party sure enough. Even I could hear it. It was on both sides. And it was after 2 A.M. that the house to the south of Mrs. Mutch turned off its lights at last.

I set my alarm for 5 A.M.

At 5:10 A.M my alarm having failed to wake me, my wife shook me awake.

"What's going on?" she demanded. "Listen!"

I hurried to my back window.

At Mrs. Mutch's lighted back door some sort of meeting was being held.

In pyjamas, dressing gowns and hastily-donned garments of one kind and another, members both young and old of both next-door families were gathered arguing with Mrs. Mutch, who was inside her screen door.

I hastened down in my bath robe and went to the back fence in the dim dawn, to partake, as they say, of the incident.

"Very well," said Mrs. Mutch, raising her voice for my benefit, "I'll turn it down a little."

"You'll turn it OFF!" commanded the father of the south family.

"Why, no," said Mrs. Mutch, very friendly and reasonable. There's no law that says there is a time limit. You like music at 2 A.M., three hours after I've gone to bed. I like music early in the morning."

The voices of a hillbilly quartet singing Down In The Valley through their noses could be heard clearly. It seemed to be coming from both sides, indeed, all four sides, of Mrs. Mutch's house.

"Turn that thing OFF!" cried the mother from the north family.

"Not at all," said Mrs. Mutch, closing the inner kitchen door and vanishing.

For a few moments, the group lingered uncertainly, talking, in the light of Mrs. Mutch's kitchen door. The younger ones were first to depart to their separate houses. I came indoors and watched from my kitchen window.

My phone rang. It was Mrs. Mutch.

"Their children have THEIR radios on too!" she said indignantly. "Both of them!"

I guess the moral of this adventure is that teenagers don't require any sleep.

The Tip

ON MY WAY to the dining car for lunch, I had to walk four cars forward.

In the second car, I overtook a tiny, elderly woman tottering ahead of me, holding on to the seat backs for support.

I excused myself and got ahead of her, so as to be able to open the doors. But at the first set of doors, we met a dining-car waiter in his white outfit coming the opposite way. He was making the second call for luncheon.

"Ah, there!" he said, holding the doors open for us.

Then he changed direction.

"Take hold of my arm, ma'am," he said to the old lady.

And for the remaining two cars, jiggling and swaying, he escorted the old lady very skilfully, and smiled us into the presence of the steward. Then he went back to his announcing job.

The steward assumed that the old lady and I were together, and sat us at a table for two.

She was a very plain old lady, and deaf, as I found out when I mentioned it was a fine day. She didn't hear me. Her purse was scuffed. Her dress was homely.

When the waiter who had helped her returned to the diner, it turned out he was our waiter. The old lady ordered, after painful scrutiny of the menu, a sandwich, a glass of milk and some ice cream. I took the fish luncheon.

She smiled at me, shyly, and mentioned it was a fine day. That was the extent of our conversation. She finished her lunch long before I had half eaten my whitefish; and when she came to pay her bill, $1.20, she looked about for some time before deciding to leave a 10-cent tip.

Our waiter thanked her cordially, and helped her free of the table. Then he gave her his arm, and escorted her. He was gone five minutes, so he must have shown her all the way to her car.

By the time he got back, the steward had seated a new passenger at my table.

This was a solid gentleman with a round bald head and shiny glasses. He had the wide-open stare of the man of action. I am pretty good, after all these years, at spotting a dining-car orator when I see one. So I signalled the steward for my bill before the new gentleman had time to more than remark that it was a fine day, to which I cordially assented.

My bill was $2.25. When the waiter came back with my change, I handed him a dollar bill.

I gave him a wink.

"On behalf," I said, "of the human race."

He winked back. I got up and left with a friendly nod to my so recently-acquired table mate. His stare was beautifully blank.

I went to the club car, seeing, in passing, the little old lady snoozing in her car.

Half an hour of beautiful scenery passed before somebody sat down in the chair next to me. It was the gentleman from the diner.

There is only one way to escape a club-car orator, and that is to have a paperback whodunit into which to be burrowed. But I had no paperback.

"Well, sir," he said, "I could not help but notice that you gave that waiter at lunch a dollar for a tip."

"That's true," I admitted.

"You'll excuse me," he said, "but this interests me very much. I am most concerned with the whole subject of tipping. I travel a great deal, and see more of this tipping evil than most people."

"Pardon me," I said, getting up to knock my pipe ashes out in one of those ash stands up the aisle.

"As I was saying," he resumed when I sat down, "this whole business of tipping is a problem we have to face. Now, I took the trouble to ask that waiter what you had for lunch. It was the fish. That came to $2.25. Right? A tip of a quarter would have been ample. That is better than 10 per cent? Right?"

"Right," said I.

"If you had given him an extra dime," he continued, "that would have been roughly 15 per cent of the bill, which is what most people seem to think is the present fashion in tipping."

"Right!" I put in first.

"What I maintain," he stated, loud enough for all those within four chairs of us to hear, "what I maintain is that tipping should be abolished, and a small service charge, if you like, included in the bill."

"They adopt that," I agreed, "in many parts of Europe."

148

"With what result?" began my orator, glasses glittering.

"With the result," I beat him to it, "that the waiters are all gloomy and sour-puss, and wait on you as if you were an inmate of an institution."

"Aw, wait, now!" protested my friend.

"Tipping," I declared, "lends a little element of excitement, mystery and adventure to the otherwise tiresome life of the waiter or the waitress. It puts a gamble into the daily task. They never know what they are going to get. Sometimes, the customer shows every evidence of being a well-heeled and generous character, and he ends up by leaving two dimes. Other times, a quite plain and unpromising customer will haul off and leave 50 cents, or even 75."

"You've hit the problem," interrupted another orator, "right on the button. The great problem in tipping is that it worries people. Nobody knows WHAT to give."

"True," said I. "But at least those in the profession of waiting on tables are inspired to give a little extra service . . ."

"There's another thing!" cried my opponent. "Those who look the part get all the service. And poor people, or unpretentious people, don't get any."

"Like little plain old ladies, for example," I mentioned.

"Eh?" said he.

"Harrumph," I said.

"Well, anyway," said he, "it is a matter of principle with me. I would like to see all tipping abolished everywhere. And in the meantime, I don't pamper them. I may tell you, having seen you give that man a DOLLAR, for doing for you what he is merely supposed to do, I gave him exactly what he deserved."

"And what was that?" I inquired.

"Nothing!" said my friend triumphantly, his eyes wide and cool. "I paid my bill, got up and walked out."

"And that," I admitted, "is not easy to do."

"Right!" said he, looking me up and down, though seated.

At this moment, our waiter appeared at the aisle of the club car. I smiled. He smiled. He surveyed the passengers and then came forward to my neighbour.

"Excuse me, sir," he said. "But have you lost anything?"

"Not," said he, calmly, "that I am aware of."

The waiter held out a wallet.

The gentleman grabbed it, snapped it open and ran a practised thumb over the bills enclosed.

"It probably fell out of your hip pocket," said the waiter, "when you got up from the table."

He turned and walked from the club car.

My neighbour shifted his wide cool gaze on me. But it was a little frazzled.

He jumped up and hurried after the waiter.

He didn't come back.

The Splash

THIS CUT over my nose?

No, no; it's not REALLY a black eye.

Ha, ha, I know, I know. You think somebody punched me on the nose?

Well, it's so silly . . . but I'll tell you about it.

You see, the restaurant where my wife and I are in the habit of having lunch every week or so has a large downstairs dining-room, and a gallery or balcony, a sort of mezzanine, that runs all around the main room.

We always go up in the balcony.

The balcony is, by custom, reserved for men only; ladies are expected only when accompanied by men.

It is a good arrangement. Downstairs, there, in the more spacious main dining-room, the women dominate. In twos and fours, all got up in their downtown lunching finery, with a good sprinkling of executive-type ladies, they gabble-gabble-gabble and slowly eat their caloried luncheons, gazing appraisingly about at one another.

But up in the balcony, the businessmen, in twos and fours, clutch cosily to their food, entirely ignoring their neighbours: a good, manly place to eat a good, manly lunch. And, here and there, you see a lady with a man.

The way I figure it, any men you might see, glancing

over the balcony, sitting down with the women in the main dining-room, are dominated men.

And any ladies you see up in the men's balcony are women who belong to men who won't put up with any flah-flah and yak-yak all around them, as they lunch on *omelette aux fines herbes,* or smelts.

Thanks to the acoustics of the place, all you can hear of the flah-flah down on the main floor is just a kindly hum.

We were shown to a table for two along the railing of the balcony. After I had politely assisted my wife to the armchair—she likes the armchair, you can rest your arms so comfortably—I sat myself down facing, by the railing, which is a fine, ornamental bronze filagree construction, affording a lofty view of the scene beneath: the scores of tables occupied by pairs and quartets of ladies, all furiously gabbling, and gazing slant-eyed at their neighbours.

"Aha!" I said, inspecting the menu with quick, accustomed eye. "Smelts!"

Fish always comes fifth on the menu.

"You never change, do you?" remarked my wife.

I removed my spectacles and set them on the railing of the balcony.

"How many times," mentioned my wife, "have I told you not to put your glasses on that railing?"

"Of course, of course!" I remembered, and reached for them.

But my eyes were taking in the prospect below, all those poor, bedecked women, fated to dwell down there in an atmosphere of eternal yak.

And my finger tips, instead of picking up the glasses, flicked them lightly instead.

They slid off the polished flat metal top of the ornamental railing.

"Good heavens!" I said.

"Exactly!" said my wife. "What I have been predicting for years."

I leaped to my feet to look over the balcony.

Directly under me was a pantomime of extraordinary activity. A gentleman and two ladies were standing up by the table, their serviettes poised before them. A fourth lady, facing the gentleman, was still sitting, leaning back and dabbing at her bosom, her lap and her chin with her napkin. Two waitresses were converging hotly on the table, napkins at the high port. And a hostess in white, her menus clutched in the approved position by her left breast, was weaving purposefully from the flank.

And all eyes, including those of people at a dozen adjoining tables, were raised at me.

An appraising glance suggested to me that my spectacles had fallen in the soup. In front of the seated lady was an unmistakable plate of what appeared to be vegetable soup, pinkish-yellowish.

Meeting all those staring faces, I motioned apologetically, and pointed urgently, with downward stabbing gestures of my index finger, at the soup plate.

My spectacles were obviously in the soup. And, of course, I should mention that they cost $24, in those frames.

"In," I framed widely with my mouth, so they could read my lips at that distance, amid all that yak, "the soup!"

But they just continued to stare up at me; and the

153

sitting lady curved herself up to get at herself better with the napkin.

"I'd better go down for them," I said to my wife.

"Oh, no doubt somebody would bring them up to you," she responded.

So I went back to the wide carpeted stairway that leads down to the main dining-room lobby, where a hostess met me.

"Are you the gentleman . . .?" she asked firmly.

"Yes," I said. "Have you my glasses? Perhaps I had better go and speak to them . . ."

"Perhaps," said the hostess, "you had better."

So I followed the hostess through the aisles of tables; and as we drew near the scene, I perceived that there was little sympathy in the expressions of those sitting around, though most of them were wearing glasses, and should know the cost of these items.

At the table where my glasses had fallen, they were still standing up, all, except the lady curved in a sort of U shape, sitting.

They glared at me.

The table, I noticed, which the waitresses were dexterously changing, cloth, plates, food and all, was splashed with soup pretty liberally.

"Have you seen my glasses?" I opened. "They have silver plastic rims . . ."

"Look, sonny," said the gentleman, who, I noted, was tall and bald and grim, rather than dominated-looking, "you and your glasses have made a pretty mess here!"

He waved his table napkin.

"My dear sir," I said, "anybody could let his glasses slip off over the railing."

154

"I say," repeated the gentleman louder, "you've made a pretty mess here!"

And he pointed dramatically at the U-shaped lady who was still curved, scrubbing at her bosom, her lap and her chin.

"Why, naturally," I agreed. "A pair of spectacles, falling into a plate of soup? What else could happen? I have always maintained that soup should be served in cups at luncheon, rather than plates."

And I leaned forward and picked up a fork and raked in the soup plate.

Sure enough, there were my glasses. I picked them delicately out.

"For two cents," said the gentleman, giving his table napkin an ill-natured shake, "I would punch you in the nose!"

No, no. Don't be hasty. He didn't punch me.

I backed away as tactfully as I knew how.

The hostess followed me out.

I started up the wide carpeted stairs.

I was polishing my glasses with my handkerchief.

At the landing of the stairs, there is a big bronze newel post.

Ornamental bronze, like the railing. With knobs on it.

I missed my footing, due to not having my glasses on. I stumbled and fell, both hands involved with the glasses, and struck my nose on the newel post.

THAT is how I got this cut on the nose.

All right, O.K.: and the black eye.

But I wasn't PUNCHED.

The Wink

AT NOON HOUR, there is an express elevator that takes customers straight to the restaurant on the top floor of the big department store. Bert Patridge and I stood back while the more important-type of our fellow citizens pushed on ahead of us. Last in, first out, is our motto.

It is our motto for good reasons. I am short. And there is humiliation in a crowded elevator, having somebody's hip pockets up against your face. Bert Patridge is tall. But he is extremely shy. He's one of those old-fashioned shy people you rarely see nowadays. He blushes with confusion if anybody even looks at him.

Maybe he gets in elevators last because he has the excessive politeness of shy people. Or maybe it is because when he is last in, nobody can look at him, and he doesn't have to look at anybody.

The elevator filled. Bert and I stepped in. The girl operator was just about to shut the doors when a man and two ladies squashed aboard.

"Well back in the elevator, please!" sang out the girl, and closed the doors.

Bert, as is his invariable custom, had removed his hat on stepping in.

Personally, I never take my hat off in elevators. That is one of those ridiculous affectations. My real reason

156

is, I don't like tall people in elevators sitting on my hat.

Oh, yes. A hat can be sat on from the standing position, in elevators.

As Bert removed his hat, these last-comers, wriggling firmly, pushed us back.

And hardly had the elevator started up before the lady squashed against Bert suddenly wrenched herself around and gave him a fierce glare. A long, fierce glare.

I glanced at Bert. He had flushed purple.

The lady shrugged and slowly turned away her accusing stare.

Bert stood with bowed head, his face burning, tears in his eyes.

When we reached the restaurant floor, the lady turned again as she stepped off and looked Bert up and down with a withering glance.

Bert stumbled off beside me. His hat was squashed flat.

"All I tried to do," he whimpered, "was rescue my hat!"

He held it up to show me.

"I just sort of pulled it out from under her," he moaned.

"Forget it, old boy," I counselled him heartily, and we went to the check room.

But when we went to our usual table, where Herriot and Cooper were already seated, Bert was still in a state of shock, still flushed, hands trembling.

"Hello?" said Herriot, concerned.

So I explained what had happened. A lady had sat on Bert's hat in the elevator, from the standing position; and Bert had unwisely tried to recover it. I described the lady's reactions.

157

"Was she a good-looker?" inquired Herriot.

"As a matter of fact," I said, "she was homely. Smartly dressed, but plain as a horse."

"Ah, that's always the way," said Herriot the connoisseur. "It's the homely ones who are always expecting to be pinched."

"I didn't PINCH her," protested Bert desperately. "All I did was just try to pull my hat from under . . ."

So we gave poor old Bert the laughter treatment, and then proceeded to turn our attention to the menu.

By the time the food arrived, we had got Bert back to his normal colour. And when Cooper mentioned that before this month of March is out, the robins will be back on the housetops, Bert became his old self. He is our champion bird watcher. We are all bird watchers; but Bert is our peerless leader. He has what we call a "life list" of over three hundred species of wild birds seen and positively identified in Canada. That may sound funny. But for most of us forty thousand bird watchers in Canada and three million in the United States, bird watching is a competitive sport that takes us out of our motor cars and makes us walk on our feet in the blessed outdoors the year round, up hill, down dale, in woods and pastures, around the lakes, through the swamps, like youngsters playing Treasure Hunt. And we vie with one another, as in any other sport, to see how many different species we can find, truly identify and proudly proclaim.

At the mention of the swift approach of spring, Bert was entirely cheered up; and we started discussing our plans for a trip in June to a heronry Bert found last summer. Here one hundred blue herons have built their ramshackle nests high in the dead trees of a little lost lake far back from the highways.

"It entails a four-mile walk," warned Bert, "through the bush. There's no trail, but I blazed the route last year."

"I'll tell you who would love to come with us," said Cooper. "Bill Calder."

"Bring him along," said Bert. "Who is he?"

"He was in my squadron in the war," said Cooper. "He lost one eye when his Spit Nine was shot down."

"A one-eyed bird watcher?" I checked.

"He can see perfectly," said Cooper. "With binoculars, he can do fine. I've had him out several times, though he's just a beginner. But that four-mile walk through the bush is what brought him to mind. He loves the bush."

"Bring him along," repeated Bert. "The more the merrier. The herons won't mind. But I can't figure how a man with vision in only one eye can focus for distance, for instance."

Bert closed one eye and put his finger out, moving it various distances from his eye.

"Hmmm," he said. "That's interesting."

We all tried it, closing one eye and glancing around at different objects.

Bert cast his one eye up at the light fixtures, at the ceiling.

He was busy experimenting in this one-eyed fashion when a departing party of lunchers passed our table.

A gentleman and two ladies.

I was too late to warn Bert.

With one eye closed, in the purely scientific inquiry of what it would be like to be a bird watcher with only one eye, Bert calmly surveyed the passing party.

159

The lady halted in her tracks.

Her companions halted.

"THAT'S the SAME man!" she shrilled, pointing a long, thin finger right at Bert.

He opened his eye.

All three of them swelled up, withered us, and then proceeded to the cashier's desk.

When, after a few moments, we had got Bert breathing normally again, he said:

"I don't think I'll go back to the office. I think I'll take a taxi home."

The Tab

I WAS ASTONISHED to see, out of the corner of my eye, Robert, our waiter, kick a child's hat under the serving table.

It was no accidental kick. It was deliberate and skilled. As he bent over the table next to ours to lay a plate of salad before one of the ladies, he caught the pretty little hat with his toe and turfed it five feet under the side table, where it disappeared.

As Robert straightened up, he caught my astonished gaze.

He winked.

I have known Robert for twenty years. We always sit at his table whenever Herriot takes me to this, his favourite restaurant. Robert is at least seventy. He has, therefore, the grace and dignity of the old-fashioned waiter, and it is a pleasure and a ceremonial to be tended by him. In fact, I regard him as one of my friends.

To see him kick a child's hat, however, was something of a shock. The hat belonged to one of three little girls who were lunching with the two Mammas at the adjoining table. It had fallen off the chair back where it had been hung with the coat. It was a cute little hat, with frills and a bit of mink, I think. Both

161

the Mammas had minks, which they had thrown over the chair backs when they sat down.

"See you later!" said Robert, bending to my ear as he put a fresh pat of butter on my side plate.

I had not paid much attention to this little hen party next to us. But now I studied them. The ladies were the mink type, typical well-to-do young matrons, easy, assured, full of chatter. The three little girls with them, from eight to twelve years of age, were the typical children of the mink type, miniatures of their mothers, entirely at their ease in a public restaurant, and carrying on their own chatter regardless of their Mammas. The little blonde one, facing me, owned the hat that Robert had kicked. She bounced around a good deal, did more reaching than was quite ladylike, and when she wasn't narrowly watching her two little friends, she was observing, with obvious distaste, the occupants of adjoining tables, including me.

I wondered if, after all, Robert was some kind of a socialist. This I had not suspected. True, I would be a little miffed if I were a waiter and were so superbly ignored by those I served, except for monosyllabic instructions in a critical tone of voice. But that, of course, is part of mink.

Yet even if I were a socialist, I would hardly kick a child's hat.

The party at the adjoining table had been there before Herriot and I were seated, and they broke up while we were half-way through the veal cutlets with strips of anchovy over them, which Herriot and I always eat when Robert waits on us. He would never bring them from the steam table. They are fresh off the fire.

As the children were being coated and hatted, I overheard the Mammas arguing as to who would pay the tab. They were still arguing as they headed toward the exit, where the cashier sits in her booth. The little girls trailed behind.

Robert was standing by the vacated table, his eyes on the exit.

I had my eyes on Robert.

When I saw a wintry smile light up his solemn visage, I glanced in the direction he was looking. There was nothing much to see.

Just the usual little bunch of people grouped while those concerned with paying the tabs were lined up.

"Now!" said Robert, coming over and whisking our table cloth corners professionally with his napkin. "Just as I figured. They've gone."

"Didn't they leave you a tip?" asked Herriot.

"No, no," said Robert, exhibiting a dollar bill. "But they forgot THIS!"

And he held up a white slip of paper.

The tab!

"It's a familiar racket," said Robert, relaxing, as old waiters are privileged to do. "Waiters are all on to it. It goes like this. As soon as they sit down, they start arguing about whose treat it is. They make sure the waiter hears them. One lady says 'No, no, darling, it is MY turn!' and the other lady says 'Nonsense, sweetheart, you paid the LAST time!' 'I didn't.' 'You did.' 'I didn't.' 'You did.' And each time the waiter arrives within hearing, there is some talk about whose turn it is to pay the tab. Didn't you hear them?"

"As a matter of fact," I admitted, "I did hear them squabbling in a pleasant sort of way about something."

"It was about the tab," said Robert. "Anyway, the

last thing they do, as they gather up their coats, is to arrive at a complete disagreement. They choose to leave when there is a crowd around the cashier. Thus, if anybody happens to notice that they have left the tab on the table, usually hidden under a plate or a table napkin, and if the waiter rushes up just as they reach the front door, they can always be most embarrassed, and one cries 'Why darling, I thought YOU had the check.' And the other can be speechless with astonishment, 'Why, my dear, I was sure YOU had it.'"

"Robert," I said, "you exaggerate."

"Not me!" said Robert. "That's why I kicked the hat under the serving table."

He stooped down, retrieved the hat and smoothed it tenderly.

"That blonde child," he said, "is the kind that won't wake up to the fact that she has no hat until they are half-way to the parking lot. She'll be too busy watching her little playmates' every move."

"Aw, Robert," I protested, fearing my old friend was a socialist after all, "people as well-off as they obviously were, people who wear mink coats, people with charming snooty little children like those, wouldn't stoop to embezzling a lunch."

Robert bowed the way waiters bowed back in the days when a tip was ten cents.

"Sir," he said, "there's quite a number of ways of getting a mink coat."

He had the hat in his hands, smoothing it, when our attention was attracted to the cashier's booth.

There were the ladies, a little flushed and flustered, inquiring.

Robert, advancing, held up the hat.

"Aaaah!" cried the ladies.

With the other hand, Robert held up the tab.

"Mercy!" cried the one lady. "Didn't YOU pay it, darling?"

"Good heavens!" cried the other lady. "I thought YOU looked after it."

They took the tab and studied it, then figured a little.

Then they both dug in their purses and paid their part.

"I should have mentioned, sir," said Robert, when the ladies had gone, pushing the little girls ahead of them, "that when trapped by a good hat-kicker or glove-pincher or scarf-filcher, they ALWAYS agree on a Dutch treat."

The Bell

"NOTHING," I agreed, "is nicer than an old farm bell at a summer cottage."

"This one I've got my eye on," said Bill Ivey, "is on an old run-down farm down a side road off the Hockley Valley."

"They're nice and old-fashioned," I reflected. "To hear them ringing across the water. They're grand for calling the fishermen home for supper, or the kids from the neighbours'."

"Awff," said Pete Lloyd, who is the crabbiest and least patient of our little group that eats lunch together, "what you want is one of these compressed-air whistles or hooters. Sirens. You can hear them miles away."

"Lovely at a summer resort," I remarked.

"This old bell," went on Bill Ivey, "is pretty rusty. It hangs kind of cocked up on its post. Maybe it doesn't ring."

"Haven't you tried it?" I asked.

"No," said Ivey. "This old farm—it's just a kind of dump—is guarded by the fiercest dog I ever met in my life. It's huge. Mixture of all the big dogs you ever heard of. And every time I've driven in the lane, it comes charging out, frothing at the mouth, baring its teeth like a mad lion."

166

"Well, didn't anybody come out of the house?" I inquired.

"No. And I toot and blow the horn, but nobody ever shows up. Just this wild animal circling the car and ravening like a pack of wolves."

"I've never met the dog yet," said Pete Lloyd, "that I couldn't handle."

"You sure couldn't handle this one," said Ivey.

"What are you doing this Saturday?" asked Lloyd.

"I hear," said Ivey, "an old man lives alone on the farm. A sort of hermit. The neighbours tell me he never comes out to meet anybody that calls."

"What are you doing this Saturday?" repeated Lloyd.

"We could leave around ten, and be in the Hockley Valley in an hour and a half."

"Personally," I said, "I am not too keen on invading old hermits' property, especially when guarded by savage dogs."

"Large dogs," added Ivey.

"Do you want that bell?" insisted Lloyd.

"I sure do," admitted Ivey. "There's darn' few of them left on the old farms of Canada."

"What do you say, then?" demanded Lloyd. "Ten A.M. Saturday?"

"I'll drive," I said.

For at this time of year, nothing is more pleasant than a lazy drive in the country, down back roads, through flower-decked valleys and up across bee-loud pastures and meadows, in search of something as unimportant, in these highly-organized days, as a rusty old farm bell dating back, probably, to the days of Sir John A.

We were about ten miles from the Hockley Valley

167

and getting ready to look for the side road that Ivey would remember, when I saw a boy on the shoulder of the highway holding up his hand in the signal for a lift.

As we came near, I saw he had a little haversack over his shoulder—obviously a boy starting on a hike.

I drew up the car.

"Awff, for Pete's sake!" said Lloyd, who had the back seat to himself quite comfortably. "A noisy kid!"

The boy got in beside him.

"Where to?" I asked.

"I got to meet my cousins, we're going on a hike," said the boy. "It's about ten miles from here."

"What's your name, son?" asked Lloyd.

"Andy," said the boy. "Andy Czernowics."

"Ah," said Lloyd, "one of these New Canadians, eh?"

"No, sir," said the boy. "My family came out in 1878 to help build the C.P.R."

"Oh," said Lloyd, whose family came out around 1920.

When in a few minutes we came to the side road Ivey was watching for, I slowed up to let the boy out.

"How much farther," I asked, "have you to go?"

"It's about two miles," said the boy. "But I've plenty of time, thank you, sir."

"Then stay in," I said. "We're only going half a mile down here, and I'll run you the rest of the way when we come out."

"Aw, for Pete's sake!" said Lloyd, who likes the back seat to himself to sprawl in.

We went the half-mile Ivey had predicted and, sure enough, came to a lane half-grown up with thorn bushes and weeds. At the end of it was the aged and sagging farm house.

And up from its door sill leaped the biggest, roughest, ugliest dog I ever saw. It came, head low, charging for the car; and you could see its teeth bared in a sneering snarl fifty feet away. Its barks and snarls, intermingled were enough to panic a tank crew.

I drove as close to the house as the lane allowed.

"O.K.," I said. "There's your dog."

Lloyd opened the car door slightly and started to speak to the dog.

It leaped as if to grab Lloyds foot, so he slammed the door shut.

"Blow the car horn," he commanded. "Keep on blowing it until the old fool comes to the door."

Ivey sounded the horn—Toot! Toot!

"I've tried it before," he said. "For ten minutes at a time. It's no good. You go and rap on the door."

But we had to yell at each other, the dog was making such a furious row.

"Go ahead, Lloyd, old bean," I urged. "Don't tell me this is the first dog you ever met that you couldn't handle."

"Well, holy Nellie," said Lloyd, "this isn't a DOG!"

The little boy piped up.

"Do you want to call at the house?" he asked.

"Now, listen, kid . . . ," said Lloyd.

"The most interesting people to a dog," said the little boy, whose great-great-grandpa had helped built the C.P.R., "is anybody eating something."

He was undoing his haversack, from which he took a newspaper package, and from it a large sandwich lined with cold roast beef.

169

He ran the car window down and peered out at the roaring dog, and took a big bite of the sandwich.

The dog's roars immediately subsided to a wild whine.

"Hi!" said the boy, leaning out and chewing loudly.

The dog ceased whining and stared with glaring eyes up at the boy.

The boy undid the door and stepped down.

The dog drew alongside him, and as the boy walked toward the house the big dog followed eagerly at his side, tail wagging.

"Come on, sir," called the boy. "To a dog, anybody that is eating is a friend."

We got out slowly, and followed the boy up to the house. The dog merely glanced at us. Its entire attention was on this lovely, chewing little boy.

Ivey rapped on the door.

After a minute, the door opened six inches and a red-eyed, stubble-faced old man glared out at us.

"I wanted to inquire," said Ivey politely, "about your farm bell. I would like to make you an offer for it."

"It isn't," said the old man, "for sale."

"Aw, for Pete's sake," said Lloyd, "EVERYTHING'S for sale if the price is high enough."

The old man gave a strange, mirthless laugh and shut the door in our faces.

So we got back in the car; the boy gave the dog a piece of the sandwich; and we drove out and I took him on to his cousin's, two miles up.

Yes, sir, I guess some things AREN'T for sale. If you've got certain things, you hang on to them.

The Detour

"AW, HECK!" I said. And drew the car to a stop at the country crossroads.

On the far right-hand corner, nailed to a post, was a crudely-lettered sign about the size of a card table:

"Keep off tar and oil."

And on the far left-hand corner, on a rail fence, was a smaller sign with a blue arrow pointing down the gravel road to the left.

"What'll we do?" asked Herriot.

There was no sign of tar or oil ahead.

"We're in no hurry," said Herriot. "You don't want to get the car all slathered up with tar and oil."

The gravel road straight before us was the familiar route we had been taking for several years as a cut-off to Blue Trout Lake. We left the paved highway twelve miles or so back. This cut-off saved us seventeen miles.

"Aw, heck!" I said.

"It's only two P.M.," said Herriot. "And it's the evening rise we're interested in. Take the detour."

"O.K. I wonder how far we've got to go around?"

"Follow the arrows," suggested Herriot.

I turned left. Not as good as the cut-off.

About a mile along, we came to another sign:

"Mulligan's Lake, 2 mi."

"Mulligan's Lake," I said to Herriot. "Never heard of it."

The next concession was a dirt road. We kept straight on.

Then we came to another hand-lettered sign.

"Visit the quilt sale at St. George's Church."

A little way on, another sign.

"Happy Holliday Motel, Mulligan's Lake, 1 mi."

And the next thing we knew, we had come over a rise of the road, and there was a little village around a small lake the size of a city block.

It was very pretty. A characteristic hamlet, with a church, a general store, a few frame houses, one brick house, a gas station and, down at the far end, a motel of eight cubicles.

"Boy, this is sweet," said Herriot.

I slackened speed.

There was quite a number of cars for so small a place. As we passed the gas station, Herriot sat up.

"Let's take a look at the quilt sale."

Most of the cars were parked around the church, and for some distance on either side. I got a parking spot.

To make a long story short, Herriot and I went into St. George's Church basement and saw the most sensational collection of home-made quilts we ever saw. There were over forty on exhibition, with several large empty spaces for those already sold.

I got one, for $22, of lady-slipper orchids, the rose and white blossoms the size of a rugby football, and the long lance-shaped green leaves three feet long—a masterpiece. And also, for $14, a quilt based on Indian designs like a Navajo rug, in grey, red and black. Herriot, who is a bachelor, got a beauty for $18 in overlapping rings of pink and pale green.

"Wow!" said Herriot. "I wouldn't have missed this . . .!"

When we were through at St. George's Church, we

172

went for a walk. At the blacksmith shop—and there aren't many blacksmith shops left—we found the front all hung with gaff hooks of every size.

"I make 'em," said the blacksmith, "out of old pitchfork tines. Busted pitchforks. A dollar."

I took two, different sizes. Herriot took two.

At the motel, we found the rooms cost five dollars a night.

"My wife," said the proprietor, "puts up some sort of breakfast if you want it. Ham and eggs. Fried potatoes."

"Any fish in the lake?" we inquired, gazing out over the little quiet water.

"Well, no," said the motel man. "It's just kind of for looking at, I guess."

"Four," said Herriot, looking at his wrist watch.

So, with a sense of regret, and the quilts in paper packages in the back seat, we bade farewell to Mulligan's Lake.

"Man," said Herriot, "what a lucky break. That tar and oil. We've been going by all these years, and never knew there was a Mulligan's Lake in here."

I backed into the service station near where my car had been parked.

"How far," I asked the service man, "do we go to get around the tar and oil?"

"Take the next road right," said he.

"Fill 'er up!" I said, drawing over to the pump.

We drove along to the right turn, another gravel road, and headed for the cut-off.

"Look," said Herriot. I'm going to phone long distance at the next place we see a phone, and tell the girls about that quilt sale. It'll be on for another day or two. They would be thrilled by it. I've never seen quilts like those, all locally made."

"Good idea," I agreed.

When we came out to the cut-off road, there was a gas station on the corner, and a blue Bell Telephone sign jutting out from the wall.

While Herriot was in telephoning the girls, I got into conversation with the service man.

Two cars came down the cut-off, from the proper direction.

"Well," I said, "they don't seem to have suffered."

"Suffered?" said the gas man.

"No tar or oil on them, by the looks of them."

"Aw," said the service man, "there isn't any tar or oil."

"No tar or oil?" I demanded, astonished.

"Naw," said he, "that's just a gimmick the boys down at Mulligan's Lake dreamed up. They're away off the main roads."

"But," I expostulated indignantly, "to put a sign up . . ."

"All it says," explained the service man, "is to keep off tar and oil. That's a good piece of advice, isn't it? You ought to keep off tar and oil."

"But," I insisted, "the arrows . . . What does the county roads department think of shenanigans like that?"

"I guess," said the service man, "they don't know about it, or something. Anyways, I see you bought some quilts."

Herriot came out.

"I gave the girls directions," he said. "They're tickled pink."

To tell the truth, so was I.

174

S O S

ON THE FAST TRAIN from Chicago to Cedar Rapids, Ia., where I was going to attend the beagle field trials, I went into the club car on the off chance that I might recognize some other beaglers.

It is funny how much like us the Americans look when they are up in Canada, and how unlike us they look on their home ground.

They are a distinct race. They dress differently, they behave differently, even in a club car; they are grave, a little solemn; they talk more importantly to one another; and if they are not talking to anyone, they make no effort to conceal their boredom.

For instance, directly across from me, about the middle of the club car, sat a middle-aged man with a briefcase clutched on his lap. He was obviously a prosperous businessman, bald, thin-necked, and with a dark burning gaze. He had his eye on me the moment I sat down. I suppose that is why I noticed him.

He looked like a sick man. He appeared feverish. And he stared so intently at me that I immediately glanced away for fear he was one of those travellers who long to relate their symptoms or misfortunes to you, mile upon mile.

On looking over the other occupants of the club car I could see no apparent beaglers. But I could feel the

175

eyes of the man opposite still upon me, so I took in his immediate neighbours.

On either side of him sat a thug. Just a plain thug. In Canada, our tough guys do not dress well. Nor do they ride in the club car. But in the States you quite commonly see these plug-uglies, these yeggs, these big, scar-faced, evil-eyed men dressed in the height of fashion, wearing expensive shoes, fat rings on their fingers, and calmly smoking cigars in the grand manner in club cars.

No wonder the feverish small man with the clutched briefcase had no desire to converse with THEM.

And they had no desire to converse with him. I realized they were together when they exchanged a word or two across his head.

But they just sat, heavily, lipping their cigars and casting slow, cold glances about them.

After half an hour, I imagined I could hear the feverish man uttering small whimpers and sighs. He seemed bottled up. *Why,* I asked myself, *doesn't the silly man change seats with one of the thugs. Why doesn't he get out of the club car and go and grieve in private in one of the chair cars ahead?*

I was entertaining myself with such idle thoughts when I noticed the man fourth along from them, to the right, watching me intently; and when I met his eyes, he smiled and beckoned me over to a newly-vacated chair beside him.

Ah, a beagler, I thought.

When I sat down:

"Martin, here," he said.

"Clark," I responded.

176

"Have you noticed," asked Mr. Martin in a low voice, "the man with the briefcase opposite you?"

"Well, yes, as a matter of fact . . ."

"He's signalling," said Martin, "in Morse. Do you read Morse?"

"Oh, only a phrase or two."

"He's been signalling SOS with his fingers on the chair arm," said Martin, low, "for the past half hour. Let's listen."

And after a moment, in a lull of the sounds in the car, I got it quite distinctly.

". . . - - - . . ."

"What the hell?"

"I've answered him," said Martin, "I think he got it. But all he does is keep on, '. . . - - - . . .'"

"The two sitting beside him," I said, "are pretty tough-looking big thugs. Very well dressed. But gangsters if I ever saw them. And they're together. I noticed them talking to each other over the little guy's head."

"I can see them reflected in the window," said Martin. "That's why I called you over. The little guy is frightened, eh?"

"He looks sick," I said. "He's frightened stiff."

And as we sat, we could again catch the intermittent drum of tapping on the chair arm . . . - - - . . .

As a stranger in the country, I told Martin I didn't want to get mixed up in any rough stuff. But he suggested we go forward and find the conductor and tell him about the SOS.

We found him in the third car ahead, sitting at the writing desk sorting his collected tickets. Rather diffidently, we explained about the SOS and the two yeggs and the small sick man with the cluched briefcase.

The conductor, an elderly, lean, grey-haired man, said:

"I'll go back and tell him there is something wrong with his tickets, and so bring him back up here, away from them. You stay here. If they follow him, I can then wire ahead for cops to meet the gentleman with the briefcase."

In a few minutes, the conductor returned, escorting the little man with the briefcase.

The big thugs did not follow.

"Thank God," said the little man, sinking into the chair at the writing desk. "You got my signal!"

And he reached out and gripped Martin's hand.

"Navy?" he asked.

"No, Air Force signals," said Martin.

"Look, gentlemen, I have to confess," said the little man. "I won $12,000 at a club in Chicago, and I have it here in my briefcase, taking it home to Omaha."

"Gambling?" asked the conductor.

"Well, yes," said the little man. "Craps. And after taking the greatest care, I get on this train. And here are these two big gangsters. I knew them instantly."

"You've seen them before? At the club?" asked Martin.

"No, no," said the little man. "But I know the type. They're after me. They know what I've got. And they'll knock me off before I get home. I didn't dare leave the club car."

"I'll tell you what," said the conductor. "You stay right in the club car. And I'll wire ahead for police to meet us at Omaha, and they'll escort you off and safe home. How's that?"

So Martin and I returned to the club car first.

The two thugs were now sitting side by side.

When the conductor brought the little man back a few minutes later, the thugs eyed him coldly as he scurried past them and took a chair at the back, across from Martin and me.

And there we sat, secure and safe and smiling, until we neared Cedar Rapids, where I had to get off.

And so did the two thugs. We all hoisted down our bags together.

The committee men who met me met them also.

They were beagle men.

One was a noted surgeon from Rochester, and his friend was a prosperous real-estate tycoon from Albany, N.Y.

We three became great buddies at the field trials.

The Secret

A THIN, scholarly-looking captain wearing spectacles halted our jeep on the side road.

"You are a war correspondent?"

"Yessir," said I.

"May I speak to you confidentially?"

I bailed out of the jeep and accompanied the captain to the ditch.

"I'm 'I' Branch," he said, meaning Intelligence. "We have found a couple of leaves torn out of a book along the road here, and we are looking for more. Would you please keep your eye open, and if you notice any, you might be good enough to stop and pick them up and bring them to Div. H.Q.?"

"Yessir," said I.

"It's an English book," said the captain, guardedly. "Leaves just torn out . . ."

"What book is it?" I inquired.

"Gibbon's *Decline and Fall of the Roman Empire*," said the captain. "You being a correspondent, and moving more freely about the area, I thought you might have more time, perhaps, than others to just keep an eye . . ."

"Why, of course," I said. "I'll make a point of it, sir."

"And, uh," said the captain, "it's a matter of security, so you will naturally not speak of this to anyone."

"Right," said I.

I got back in the jeep and, as we bumped and jogged along the roads of Normandy, in the wake of the troops, I found myself in the curious situation of watching along the verges of the roads of Gaul for leaves torn out of Mr. Gibbon's famous classics, *The Decline and Fall*.

I knew, of course, what was cooking.

The secret service in wartime has all kinds of tricks for communicating with friendly agents behind the enemy lines. And one of them is to use a book as the basis for passing messages.

For instance, one of Mazo de la Roche's Jalna novels was the medium of communication, the code book, by which the secret service on our side kept contact with a group of agents in occupied France.

It works like this. The two wishing to correspond in secret agree on a book, making sure they have the same edition. It should be a book likely to be found in any sizable library, not too familiar, nor too unfamiliar.

Then all they have to do is transmit a series of numbers, by radio, or on bits of paper, or even memorized for oral transmission, like this: the first number or series of numbers, followed by a zero, are the page; the next numbers, followed by the zero are the line; and the last numbers, followed by zero, are the word. Then come two zeros to make the end of the word.

To read the recipient just opens his book, checks the page, lines and words. And there's the message.

Imagine, therefore, the suspicions of Intelligence when, as the Canadians moved into Normandy and toiled their way past Caen, somebody noticed a leaf torn out of a book in English.

How strange, in such a place, at such a time, to find in the mud on the roadside of Normandy random pages ripped from *The Decline and Fall*!

Whoever first found one mentioned it to somebody else. And when somebody else, a day or so later, in another place, found more pages, the matter came to the attention of an officer of a suspicious nature, of whom there is always one in every battalion.

And in an instant, the hunt was on.

Within a week, in far scattered places on the battle-field, more pages from *The Decline and Fall* were picked up by alerted Intelligence. The riven sheets were studied minutely for marks or signs, of which there were plenty, though not very intelligible since the pages had blown in the wind and the night, the mud and the rain. On some were pencil marks and scrawls entirely undecipherable.

One question was: If the mysterious distributor of these pages was an agent, why was he destroying the book, a few pages at a time? Should he not keep the book intact in order to send and decipher his messages?

In answer was the fact the ancient University of Caen was right in the middle of the battlefield. Copies of *Decline and Fall* would certainly be fairly numerous among a population that is much more familiar with English than those in other parts of France. These torn sheets were undoubtedly some refinement of the code.

Me, I never did find one of them, though being very short, in a jeep or out of it, I had more chance of spotting one of them in the dust and the ditch than most of us.

Some three weeks later, I encountered the thin scholarly captain in the glasses. I asked him about *The Decline and Fall*.

"Oh, *that!*" he said.

"Did you find many more pages?" I inquired.

"We found them all," he said. "By tracing the location of the various units that had passed over the areas in which the sheets were found, we narrowed it down. Finally we got our man."

It seems there was a young university student who had interrupted his studies to enlist. Finding the soldiering life, even in battle, a little tedious, he had brought on the invasion with him a copy of Volume One of a three volume set of Gibbon's opus. Thus, in the quiet hours, he could retire from the filth and futility of war into the stately prose of Gibbon and the noble story of the ancient times.

But, being a soldier, and a private one at that, he was duly impressed with certain basis principles of the military life, one of which he expressed as follows to the triumphant Intelligence officers who finally ran him to earth.

When they demanded, very shrewd, why he tore the pages out of his book, he replied:

"Sir, that Volume One weighs three pounds. Why should I carry it after I've read it? So as soon as I have read the next few pages I tear 'em out, thus reducing the weight of my pack."

He produced the book.

"See?" he said. "It only weighs about half a pound now."

As far as I know, no record of the identity of this young scholar was kept.

Maybe this story will find him.

Will he be a scholar now, or a businessman?

Whichever, he will be good.

Escapists

THIS is no time of year to be lost in your car on the country back roads. And I was lost.

All I had to do, of course, was turn in any of the farm lanes and ask my way back to terra firma. But each lane I came to was so mired and rutted that I decided against the risk of getting stuck. I hooted my horn and hallooed at a couple of the farm houses that were not too far back off the road. But this is also the time of year when everybody in the country seems to be in hibernation.

I was disappointed, too. I had failed to find any ruby-crowned kinglets. One of my fellow bird watchers had telephoned me in great excitement that he had seen five ruby-crowned kinglets in a woodlot northwest of the city, and if I hustled out there, I might get in on the find.

The only reason this creates any excitement among the brotherhood is that the ruby-crowned kinglet, a little bird smaller than your thumb and weighing about the same as a ten-cent piece, does not normally appear in these parts until around April twentieth. In fact, the earliest dates in our records are around the sixth or seventh of the month. To see one earlier would be a matter of pride, like being the first to shoot a space ship at Mars, not Venus.

Aw, I know, I know! It does sound silly for a man to be lost in the mud while out trying to see a bird not much bigger than a stuffed olive. You explain it. I can't.

Well, hang it all, if I kept on going straight in one direction, instead of turning off to the right or left on every stretch of solid gravel I came to, I was bound to come out to a pavement. I was only thirty miles from town. Any minute I would meet another car.

Then I met it.

A nice big, new-model, light-blue car. It was stopped at an intersection of the road I was on and a concession crossroad.

As I approached, the driver opened his door and stepped out, raising his hand.

He was a middle-aged and formal looking gentleman.

"Good day," I said. "Is this the way out to the highway?"

"About three miles straight ahead," said the gentleman, putting his hand on the window ledge. "Look here, I was wondering if you would be good enough to drive my wife and me up this side road a mile or two."

"Well, uh . . ." I hesitated.

"My car's acting up," he said, "and if you had the time . . ."

"Well, hop in," I suggested, "and I'll drive you out to the highway where there will be a service station."

"No, no!" said he firmly with the air of one accustomed to having his suggestions accepted. "It's only a matter of a mile or so, and five or ten minutes while my wife and I look at a farm. I will gladly pay you a dollar or two for your trouble."

"Actually," I replied, "I have to get back to the city."

"Come, come!" said the gentleman. "Be reasonable. It's just up this side road a short distance."

He waved to his wife to come on.

She was one of those slim middle-aged ladies with the hard cheekbones of those who diet religiously and are very active socially. She minced across the ridgy mud and the puddles.

"Whoo!" she said. "You're all muddy! I'll sit in the back."

"I've been in woodlots," I explained, walking around. The man got in beside me.

"It's awfully good of you," said the lady kindly, "to give us a lift."

"I'm paying him a couple of dollars," said her husband briefly.

"You live around here?" asked the lady.

"No," I said, "I'm from down country."

As I turned my car into the concession road, I perceived that if I had been in the mud so far, I was certainly up to the neck in it now. The ruts, deep and chocolatey, wandered from one side of the road to the other. Dark pools concealed the ruts. A little way ahead, I could see where somebody had put some fence rails in the ruts and they projected in a random fashion.

I stopped the car.

"Oh, DO go on!" cried the lady.

"Unless," I proposed, "you have some URGENT reason . . ."

"My heart is SET," cried the lady, "on seeing this farm. It's a DARLING little old farm house, with big elms, and an orchard on BOTH sides . . ."

"You're crazy, Mary," said the gentleman beside me. "Six months of the year you'd be stuck like this."

186

"Aw, PLEASE go on!" wailed the lady, giving me a prod on the shoulder with her finger. "I've been look-forward to this for years. It's only three miles."

"Three?" said I.

"Mary," remarked the gentleman, "you're nuts!"

"Then," said the lady, "we'll go in OUR car!"

"Not a foot!" said the gentleman.

I heard the rear door open. The lady flung out, slammed my door and stamped across the ruts and puddles. She got in the back of their car.

"Pardon me," I said to the gentleman. "But what is all this?"

"My wife," said he, "has reached the age at which she thinks she would like to buy a farm not too far from the city and retire to the life of the country gentry."

"Ah."

"She has been reading these magazines devoted to gracious living," said he. "Converting old farm houses into little jewels."

I was backing my car on to the other road. "Can I," I asked, "give you a lift out to the highway?"

"What for?" he said.

"A service station," I replied. "Your car?"

"Oh, my car's all right," he said. "I just didn't want to get it all muddy up there."

He opened the door and eased himself out with slow dignity. He gave a little flip of the hand as a gesture of gratitude or farewell. He got in his car without look-ing at the back seat where his wife sat in a corner with her shoulder high. I waited until he started, turned and led out toward the highway.

I waited, fortunately, a moment longer. To think about country life, and all the people who yearn for it; and about gentry, and the sort of people who aspire to that rank; and of escape, escape from cities, escape from wives, from husbands, from one another. And how amid all the mud and the changing seasons and the concrete streets of cities and the foul broken side roads of the country, and winter coming. and winter going, we dream of escape to some happy land, far, far away.

And their car had gone out of hearing and all was quiet save for the murmur of my engine when, amid the bare lifting trees of the woodlot around me, I heard the magic sound.

You would think it was a bird as big as an oriole, a great, strong-throated, ringing bird.

"Will-EET-cha! Will-EET-cha! Will-EET-cha"

I turned off the engine.

I eased the far door open, crept out.

Wonderful stillness!

Then the tiny, rippling. trilling arpeggio that precedes the ringing cry.

I lifted my binoculars to my eyes.

"Will-EET-cha! Will-EET-cha! Will-EET-cha!"

I HAD him!

In the tip top of a maple, a tiny creature not much bigger than a stuffed olive, the ruby crown.

The Shillelagh

IT WAS my neighbour, Murphy, from around the corner. "Excuse me," he said, "but have you got such a things as a shillelagh?"

"A WHAT?" I double-checked.

"A shellaly, shilalah, shellala, or whatever you call it," said Murphy, leaning on the door jamb. "You know— one of those Irish clubs."

"I'm afraid I haven't," I confessed. "Come in, man."

"I've seen you with different sticks," said Murphy, "and I though maybe you'd have a shillelagh. I've got to appear at an Irish concert tonight, and I've got everything for my costume but one of those things."

"I haven't seen one in years," I said. "Everybody who used to visit Ireland brought one home!"

Murphy came over and sank on the chesterfield.

"My wife got me into this," he said gloomily. "Her name was O'Neill before we were married."

He apparently thought this explained everything.

"The women at the church," he said, "dreamed up this concert for St. Patrick's Day, and they got all us men mixed up in it."

"What kind of an act are you in?" I inquired.

"I'm singing," said Murphy, very hollow. "I'm wearing a green hat my wife fixed up by sewing green on to one of my old fedoras. I've got a green coat that belongs

189

to HER green tweed suit. And I'm wearing a cut-off pair of tight blue jeans tucked into golf stockings."

Murphy shuddered.

"What song are you singing?" I asked.

"Come Back To Erin," said Murphy, "Mavourneen!"

"Well," I reasoned, "what do you need a shillelagh for, singing a song like that?"

"It's my wife's idea," said Murphy.

"Well, then," I suggested, "why not rig one up from cardboard or corrugated paper and stain it?"

"I tried that," said Murphy. "But it all flew apart when I was rehearsing."

"I've got it!" I cried. "You know that lilac bush I had cut down last fall? Some of the wood is still piled at the foot of the garden."

Out we went, and found a perfect hunk of lilac root that, with a little sawing and trimming, and doused with black ink, would make as fearsome a shillelagh as ever came out of the Distressful Isle.

While Murphy and I were whittling at it down in my cellar, I came to the conclusion that I would like to hear Come Back To Erin, Mavoureen, sung with gestures and a shillelagh.

"Why, sure!" said Murphy. "I'll pick you up around 7:30. My wife's going to be up at the church hall all afternoon. Are you Irish?"

"No," I confessed. "My family came from the Hebrides."

When he arrived at 7:30, I could tell he was agitated.

"Where's the outfit?" I asked.

"There's the shillelagh on the back seat," said Murphy, "My wife took my clothes in a suitcase."

I admired our handiwork on the back seat. It was

190

bigger and blacker than any shillelagh I had ever seen. The head of it was the size of a grapefruit.

Murphy drove rather fast, with several violent jerks, as we went the five blocks over to the main street.

"Take it easy," I suggested.

"Awffff!" exploded Murphy. "I can't sing worth sour apples!"

"Why, man," I protested. "You've got a fine voice. Come on. Let's hear you."

As we turned up the main street, Murphy began in a plaintive voice.

"Louder!" I encouraged. "Let it out!"

He put some wind into it.

"Fine!" I shouted. "A little more expression!"

He was putting heart, lungs and diaphragm into it when we came to the main crossing, with stop lights. Several cars were halted ahead of us. As Murphy reached the best note in the whole song, we went slam into the rear end of the car in front of us. Not a severe bump, but a noisy one.

The two occupants of the car bailed out and came around to Murphy's window. A policeman, who had been at the corner, came to my window.

"Your brakes fail?" asked the driver of the other car.

"No," said Murphy. "I . . . uh . . ."

"What were you yelling about, then?" asked the constable in my window.

"I was not yelling," said Murphy.

"I could hear you distinctly," said the constable.

He looked in the car and saw the shillelagh.

"What's that?" he inquired, sharply.

"It's part of my costume," said Murphy. "I'm singing in an Irish concert up at the . . ."

191

"Your driver's licence, please," said the constable.

Murphy felt for it.

"I've changed my clothes so many times today," he said, "I must have left it on the dresser."

"Pull over here to the curb," said the constable.

And the two gentlemen we had bumped were instructed to pull over too.

Traffic, being cleared, moved on. And the four of us got out as the constable drew out his book and pencil.

"Your name?"

"Terence Mulvaney Murphy," said Murphy, and gave his address.

I gave mine.

"Your name?" he asked the driver of the bumped car.

"Just put it down Scissors," he said.

"Spell it," said the constable.

"C-z-y-s-c-z-e-r-s-k-y," spelled the gentleman, adding his initials and address.

"Yours?" said the constable to the other passenger.

"Colquhoun," said he.

"Spell it."

"C-o-l-q-u-h-o-u-n," said the gentleman.

After noting the numbers of both cars, the constable said we might drive on.

"Excuse me, Constable," said Murphy, "but could I have your name?"

"Certainly," said he. "It's Hohenschlinger."

Murphy was stone silent as we drove, with painful caution, the five more blocks to the church.

We were a little late arriving at the church hall. Mrs. Murphy, née O'Neill, was waiting and rushed Murphy off to a dressing room. I went and got a seat.

It was a grand concert. Children's groups singing; Irish fairy tales; Irish dancers in small shawls, their arms dangling, but their feet fluttering like little silver moths. Male quartets, solo sopranos, all rejoicing in the woes of Erin.

And when Murphy appeared, waving our shillelagh, he practically loosened the plaster of the church hall in a magnificent bull baritone as he invited us one and all to get the heck back to Erin and out of this mixed-up country full of heathen from heaven knows where.

Yoicks! Tally-ho!

IT WAS thinly snowing. Even before I saw this car pulled off to the side of the highway, I knew I was a fool to be out driving on a day like this. Hardly anybody else was out. A few trucks boring through the haze. An occasional car huddling past.

The snow was flying horizontal.

Sometimes I doubt my own common sense.

As I approached the car on the shoulder, I could see a man in the act of stooping to get in the back seat.

Then, when I was only fifty yards away, to my consternation, the car gave a violent spring forward. The man in the act of entering leaped back.

And suddenly there he was, wildly waving at me to stop.

It was at the intersection of a country crossroad. Skidding, I pulled to the shoulder.

"Quick!" he shouted, running to pull my door open. "Follow that car!"

"Well, uh . . ." I remarked.

"My wife!" gasped the man, throwing himself into the seat and slamming the door. "My wife's in that car! They drove off . . ."

As I stepped on the gas, I could see the fleeing car already far ahead and just vanishing in the grey murk.

194

"Look," I said, as I pushed down, "I'm not a very fast driver."

"Step on it!" cried the man.

He was a big, ruddy fellow in his forties. He had on a short coat and a leather cap. A farmer, likely.

He was bent forward peering through the windshield as the wiper swiped back and forth.

"I see it!" he gritted. "We're gaining!"

"What happened?" I inquired, gripping the wheel.

"Why," said the man, "I was just starting to get in . . ."

"Yes, I saw that," I said. "You're wife . . . ?"

"She got in first," said the man, eyes glued ahead, "and I was just starting to . . ."

"Look, my friend," I said in a high voice. "I'm going twice as fast as I usually go. Don't you think we had better pull up at the next village, or a gas station, and telephone ahead to the police?"

"I don't know the licence number," said the man. "Keep going! We're gaining!"

It didn't seem to me we were gaining. A couple of times we drew almost within sight of it enough to hope we could catch the licence number.

"Get its number!" I gasped, pushing down hard.

But each time, the fugitive put on a burst of speed and became once more a dim shape in the thin blizzard.

A gas station loomed up.

"Don't stop! Don't stop!" pleaded the big fellow, so forsaken.

"I just thought," I said, "maybe we might find somebody, a faster driver."

A couple of miles past the gas station, I could see for myself that we were actually gaining.

The fleeing car turned into a side road.

"I'll never keep up," I protested, "on a side road. I don't want to skid into a ditch."

"Turn!" cried the man. "Turn!"

I turned; and there, no great distance ahead, was the other car jouncing and bouncing along the rough country road.

"We've got 'em!" shouted the man.

And we had.

Second by second, I drew closer.

"Get the licence number!" I commanded.

We were now so close on the tail of the car that I could see the faces of two women and a man staring out the back window.

My heart was pumping.

"In the glove compartment," I directed, "there's a wrench. You'd better get it out in case there is any trouble."

The car ahead slowed so that I almost collided with it.

It turned into a farm lane.

I braked.

"Aren't you going in?" asked the man.

I prefer to watch fights from a little distance.

"I'll wait for you here," I said. "You go and get your wife."

"Aw," said the man.

So I turned and drove boldly up the lane.

When we reached the farmhouse, the other car was emptying. Three women, laughing cheerfully, were shaking themselves down. Three large men emerged and stood watching calmly as we drew nigh.

My man bailed out when I stopped.

"Hi," he called.

196

"Fast work," replied the man who had been at the wheel.

The women were walking toward the farmhouse.

"Come on in," said my man as he closed my door, "and have a cup of tea."

I was speechless.

"What," I finally got out, "is this?"

"Aw," said my man, "just a little fun. They were picking us up back at the corners, and it was too crowded with me in it. So I just . . ."

My gorge rose.

"You deliberately," I cried, "deliberately fooled me into thinking . . ."

He had bright and mischievous but hard blue eyes. You don't often find mischievous men who are big. But when you do, they're the worst kind.

"Why," I said bitterly, "I could have crashed, or skidded off the road!"

"Look," said the big fellow through the window, "you'd have done it for me if it had been for real, wouldn't you?"

"Well, yes," I agreed. "Of course."

"Well, what's the difference, if it was for fun?" said he. "Come on in and have a cup of tea, and we'll tell the folks about it."

Heck!

So I went in. And it was the old-fashioned sort of farmhouse, with no new plywood lining, and no kitchen full of big white appliances. And the gathering were all old-fashioned farmers, full of politeness and shyness and laughter. And they enjoyed the story about our chase with great hilarity.

197

When I happened to mention that what I was doing out driving on such a mean day was going to pick up some unpasteurized honey at a farm twenty miles farther up the highway.

"Unpasteurized!" they all exclaimed. "Why, that's the only kind! We've got a whole shed full of it."

After four cups of tea, three pieces of different cake, one piece of plum-preserve pie with criss-cross pastry top, and one bun, I drove home with six pounds of unpasteurized honey, the snow had stopped, and spring was almost in the air.

Matches

A GOOD twenty-five minutes before departure time, I boarded the afternoon train and found my reservation in the chair car, Chair 17, Car 64.

I like to be on time. In fact, I was the first passenger in Car 64. I like to have what the generals call room for manoeuvre. Maybe, for instance, my taxi driver, ten minutes away from the station, gets into a collision with another car. It would take fifteen minutes for him to finish arguing, and there I'd be. Or maybe there might be a big fire in the downtown area, with traffic backed up in all directions.

Or maybe . . .

Anyway, I like to be ahead of time.

Car 64 filled up quietly in the next few minutes. Elderly ladies arrived with fifteen to twelve minutes to spare. Mothers with six-year-old children arrived with six minutes to spare. Then, with a rush, all the really efficient types arrived, with two minutes to spare, the executives, the smoothies, the kind of people who know that the afternoon train wouldn't DARE to leave without them.

And all at once, just as the train squeaked, there loomed above me a tall, dark man with a forty-dollar briefcase and he said:

"I'm sorry, but you are sitting in my chair."

199

I scrambled up from the recumbent posture I adopt in chair cars and got out my ticket envelope.

I studied my ticket.

"Chair 17, Car 64?" I queried.

The tall dark gentleman studied his ticket.

"Chair 17, Car 64," he read, calmly.

He was, I saw, one of those calm, commanding types. Big industry and large business are full of him. He knows from long experience that all stupidities are on the part of somebody else. And the thing to do is remain calm and commanding.

"What," he asked me, as I stood up, "is the date of issue? Marked on the back. That will settle the matter."

I read the back of my ticket.

"September twenty-eight," I read.

"Let me see," he said, taking my ticket from my hand.

The porter arrived.

"Appears," said the calm, dark gentleman, putting his briefcase in the chair I had just vacated, "to be a mix-up. This gentleman has a reservation I had made."

However, I watched my ticket and took it from his hand, though he attempted, I think, to switch it for his.

The porter took the two tickets and studied them.

"Why," he said, "this is for yesterday, September twenty-seven!"

He handed the tall dark gentleman his ticket.

"Now, now," said the tall man, "there must be some mistake. My secretary got my transportaion. I told her distinctly, Wednesday, September twenty-eight."

The porter shrugged his shoulders.

"Sorry," he said. "I checked this other gentleman's ticket when he arrived."

The train quietly got under way.

200

The calm, commanding gentleman remained calm and commanding.

"Very, well," he said, with a glance around at me, the porter and any other passengers who might be interested. "Get me some other accommodation."

"You'll have to see the parlour-car conductor," said the porter.

I sank back thankfully into Chair 17.

Chair 18, directly opposite me, was vacant.

"I'll sit here," said the tall gentleman.

And as he relaxed into 18, he gave me the sidelong glance one uses, in such circumstances, on all those stupid people on which high-level management, known as the Brass, has to rely.

I filled my pipe.

They allow smoking in the chair cars now.

I tucked the tobacco in, not too loose, not too tight, and got a match from the side pocket in my jacket.

I held it up, put my thump nail against the head, gave it a jag, and the match blazed obediently.

"Good heavens!" burst out the tall dark gentleman opposite. "Never, never do that!"

"What?" I asked.

"Never," said No. 18, "strike a match with your thumb nail like that. It's most dangerous. I knew a man, old golfing friend of mine, who used to do that. I warned him repeatedly. But one fine day, he got a bit of burning sulphur off the head of the match under his thumb nail. A most agonizing experience. And he was laid up, with infection, for six weeks at the height of the golfing season."

I held the match to my pipe and got it going.

The fragrant aroma of good Scottish navy cut wafted around my head.

"What's that you're smoking?" inquired No. 18.

I think, having failed to dominate in the matter of Chair 17, he was groping around for other fields to conquer.

"A rare," I said, blowing a cloud at him, "Scottish navy cut. Cut cake, they call it. But it's a navy cut."

"Very heavy," said No. 18, reaching into his pocket and producing a good-looking pipe, straight grain, the kind that lends an air to directors' meetings.

From a black sealskin pouch, he filled his pipe.

"Mixture," he said. "Blended to a formula I came across in London."

The parlour-car conductor, followed by the porter, arrived. "May I see your ticket?" he asked.

No. 18 obliged.

"Yesterday," said the conductor.

"You can fix me up," said No. 18, "in some other car? Or how about this one?"

"No, this one's taken," said the conductor, studying his chart, "at our first stop, in twenty minutes. And I'm sorry, there isn't another chair."

"Oh, now, come, come!" said No. 18.

"Sorry," said the conductor, who appeared to be far less fearful of big shots than I am. "The porter will carry your bag forward to the coaches. They're not crowded this afternoon."

"Now, just a MINUTE!" exclaimed No. 18, slapping his hand most emphatically on his thigh. "I am not in the habit of riding in day coaches."

I smelled something funny.

202

"Wow!" yelled No. 18, springing to his feet.

He was slapping his lap and thigh frantically. Wisps of curious-smelling smoke were puffing off his trousers with every slap.

"Hey! Hoy! Quick!" he shouted.

The porter led him hastily in the direction of the end of the car labelled in gilt: "MEN."

The conductor, to confirm everything, looked at my tickets.

"Nobody," he said, as he handed my tickets back, "should carry matches in his pants pocket. Sooner or later, they scratch together, and BOOM! I once burned myself in a most distressing . . ."

The porter came back and picked the briefcase off Chair 18 and a costly cowhide bag off the rack.

And I didn't see my calm acquaintance until six hours later, at the end of the run, where he was ahead of me in the station, walking slightly bow-legged.

Decoys

AS FOR duck shooting, you can have it.

Charlie Marlin had me on the phone for half an hour.

"Look," he said, "I've got the whole thing planned down to the last detail. "It's foolproof."

"Charlie," I said, "I gave up duck shooting five years ago. You ought to remember."

"We didn't have it planned right that time," argued Charlie. "There's more to duck shooting than firing a gun. You've got to organize it. You've got to be smart. Now, this time . . ."

"Let me refresh your memory," I interrupted. "You gave me the same line you're giving me now. We got up to Mudcat Marsh the night before, and slept in our car. It was raining, remember?"

"The weather forecast for tomorrow," said Charlie, "is perfect. Southeast winds, fifteen to twenty miles. Perfect."

"All cramped and sleepless," I continued remorselessly, "we crawled out in the rain and walked a mile in hip rubber boots to the edge of the marsh before daybreak. And then you couldn't remember where your blinds were. So we sloshed around in the marsh for over an hour, disturbing about two hundred other duck shooters crouched in THEIR blinds . . ."

"All that," protested Charlie, "is ancient history. I . . ."

"Those other hunters," I reminded him, "were ready to shoot US for scaring off the ducks."

"This place I'm taking you THIS time," stated Charlie, "isn't remotely like Mudcat Marsh. It's a little lake, about a mile long . . ."

"Charlie," I cut in, "it is five years since that last trip. The number of duck hunters has not merely doubled and trebled in those five years. It has exploded. Everybody and his uncle is out with a gun nowadays. There are newcomers to the sporting scene who haven't the foggiest notion of how to shoot, let alone behave. They blast off at ducks two hundred yards away. They scare all the ducks over the U.S. border a month ahead of time. And if anybody DOES hit a duck, forty guys charge out after it, claiming they shot it."

"WILL you listen?" begged Charlie.

And he outlined a very seductive programme. His uncle's farm, not sixty miles from town, runs back to a small, wandering marshy lake with a river running through it.

"We'll sleep and eat at your uncle's?" I checked.

"Right!" cried Charlie, knowing he had me hooked. "And I've got four young cousins, between the ages of fifteen and twenty-one. They are all at the farm. Now listen to this! I'm outfitting each of them with four boxes of shells. They have two guns at the farm. You can bring that spare one of yours . . ."

"They shoot the ducks for us," I exclaimed, "while we sit around the kitchen stove in the . . ."

"No, NO!" protested Charlie. "This is where I am putting a little brains into duck hunting. The north

205

end of the lake is no good at all. So, before daybreak, I am sending my four young cousins up to the north end of the lake, with instructions to blast off, and keep shooting, at five-minute intervals, until their boxes of shells are exhausted."

"I don't get it," I admitted.

"Don't you see?" said Charlie. "There will be maybe fifty other duck hunters on the lake. When they hear all that shooting up at the north end, they'll sit there listening for about twenty minutes; and then they'll hustle up to where all the shooting is.

"And there we'll be," triumphed Charlie, "down at the south end, the good end, with practically the whole place to ourselves!"

"We split the cost of those shells?" I figured.

"It's a small price to pay for a little privacy on a duck marsh," pointed out Charlie. "I'm taking that old gun of mine to lend the boys, and you bring your spare for them. I'll pick you up after supper."

Aw, well, that is the trouble with having exuberant, overwhelming friends.

Nostalgia is a pleasant sensation. I enjoyed groping around in the attic cupboards for canvas coat, hip boots, forgotten sweaters. I tried my guns to my cheek, and decided which one to lend to Charlie's cousins.

It was nostalgic too, to listen to Charlie all the way up to his uncle's farm, exulting on the morrow.

They have a thing called "lunch" on farms. It is a snack before you go to bed. It consists of pie, fresh buns, slices of bread off home-made loaves nearly a foot high, home-made cherry jam, not to mention plum jam with a touch of cloves in it. Meat, if you want it. Cold roast pork, or beef, maybe, or ham cured right there on

206

the job. I did all right before bedtime, and was much impressed by the four young cousins of Charlie. They were wonderful eaters.

I was routed out around 4:45 A.M.

We had coffee, toast and plum jam, a few slices of crisp bacon, a couple of buns, two pieces of pie ("You don't want to catch your death of cold," explained Charlie's aunt) and a couple of boiled eggs.

Charlie led me down to the shore at the back end of the farm, where his uncle had a blind built for us, with a pail of hot embers on wet sand to keep our feet warm. The blind has a shelf for us to rest our elbows, and foam-rubber cushions on the bench.

Out on the water, thirty yards away, were the decoys the boys, routed out at four A.M., had set out for us. The poor, dull-witted ducks, prey of intelligent man, would come curving in on the fresh east wind, set their wings, stiff, and float down, easy targets.

The east wind was on the backs of our necks, ideal for duck shooting. It beat down our spines, hummed on our kidneys.

At break of day we heard a few random shots.

And, from the north end of the lake, we heard a sudden tattoo, a veritable Passchendaele of gunfire.

"Heh, heh, heh!" said Charlie.

We watched shrewdly into the murk of dawn.

Three or four ducks, singles, swept past, far out of gunshot.

Charlie nudged me. "Don't snore!" he whispered.

I blinked my eyes rapidly, and stared into the increasing day.

Five ducks came for our decoys before eight A.M. Charlie fired at four, I took on one. We missed them all, due to mathematical considerations I need not dwell upon. From the north end of the lake, the tattoo continued unabated.

At 8:30 A.M., Charlie's uncle came down with the car.

"The boys," he said, in the local idiom, "done fine. They got their count. Come on home for breakfast."

For breakfast, we had . . . uh . . . well, you know; anyway, we decided to have a little snooze. So we lay down until noon, when lunch was called.

And around three, Charlie and I headed for home, with four mallards each, from the boys, out of gratitude for the free shells and the loan of the guns.

The Wedding Party

ON THE HIGHWAY ahead, a string of eight or ten cars was halted. On either side of them off the pavement, a police car was drawn up.

"Awfff!" snorted old Dandy Daniels beside me. "Cops!"

Dandy, who is away up in his eighties, has a scunner against almost everything, but especially the police. Sergeants in particular.

"Drive past!" commanded Dandy.

I had the old boy out for this Saturday afternoon drive in the country to see the grain fields marching toward the harvest, the corn fields brightly rustling, the orchards beginning to be heavy.

In the back seat, Hortense, Dandy's old housekeeper, who has been looking after him forty years and more, was blissfully sleeping, her hearing aid removed.

"Go on, drive past!" yelped Dandy.

But I got in line; and in a minute, two provincial policemen glanced in at us and waved us on our way. I could hear the radios in the two police cars squawking busily.

A hundred yards up the highway, a car was pulled on to the shoulder, and I drew up long enough to ask:

"What's going on?"

"Been a bank holdup," called the driver, "in a town over on the next highway."

"On a Saturday?" I exclaimed.

But I had to drive on, as cars behind me were tooting.

"Yah!" said Dandy. "They'll never get 'em."

Three or four miles up the highway, I turned on to a paved side road that would take us into a pleasant agricultural district I am familiar with; and we toddled along, pausing every few hundred yards to let Dandy feast his eyes on a particularly handsome crop of corn or apples.

On topping a rise, we saw ahead of us another police car drawn up at a bridge. As we neared, we could see the provincial constable questioning people in two cars he had stopped.

"The heck with him," said Dandy. "Go right past. He has no right interfering with honest . . ."

But as I reached the bridge, I drew off on to the shoulder to inquire about this Saturday business. How do you hold up banks on Saturday, when they're closed? I showed the constable my newspaper police pass and got out. From the police car across the road came the squawking of their radio, a second constable sitting in the car with it.

"Town," said the constable at the bridge, "about twenty miles over. Hold-up gang shanghaied the manager from his home and made him open up the bank."

"No time lock?" I checked.

"A small bank, said the constable, "old-fashioned."

"Yah," called Dandy from my car. "You'll never catch 'em! Never do!"

No cars coming, the young constable strolled over and rested his elbow on the car door.

"Yah," said Dandy.

"Well, Dad," said the blue-eyed constable, with a flush around his eyes, which is always a bad sign in policemen, "you don't seem very confident in your police, eh?"

Old Dandy, his grey eyes flinty, just stared in silence at the young constable. The young constable stared back. But Dandy won.

The constable walked over to the bridge, hitching his belt.

In the distance, we could hear car horns blowing.

There was a rise ahead, and just as a car came into view, two cars, pink and white ribbons streaming from them, and their horns blowing harmoniously with the persistence familiar to these wedding flights, drew abreast of it; and the leading car made way for them.

Down the slope the two came, ribbons streaming.

The constable held up his hand, and the cars slithered to a stop.

From the front one, the most-decorated one, a flushed young man with that look of guilt characteristic of all bridegrooms, stuck his head out, wide-eyed.

Beside him sat the bride, covered with the usual confusion. In the back seat, another young fellow, in a stiff collar and a rosy flush.

"O.K.," called the constable, as he walked to the second car.

In it were two girls and two young fellows, full of the look of mischief.

"O.K.," repeated the constable, with a grin.

Horns hooting, away the cars sped.

"Hi!" called Dandy from my car.

He was crooking his finger at the constable.

"Come here, boy!" he commanded.

The constable walked over and again rested his elbow on the door to stare down blue-eyed at Dandy.

"If I were a bank robber," said old Dandy, "do you know what I would do?"

"I can well imagine," said the constable.

"I'd stash a couple of cars," said Dandy, "a couple of miles away from the job, up a side road and down a lane. I'd have my girl friends in them, all dressed up pretty, with roses in their hair. And while me and my pals were sticking up the bank, the girl friends could be busy with pink and white paper, up that lane, dressing up the cars."

The young constable straightened and glared down at Dandy.

"Yep," said Dandy, "and when we did the job me and my pals would drive like blazes, in a stolen car, probably, the couple of miles to where the girls were waiting, up a lane, and then . . ."

"Holy smoke!" shouted the constable, starting for the police car on the far side of the road, from which the sounds of the radio came rasping furiously.

He spoke to the other constable, and the squawking abruptly ceased.

The seated constable was speaking into his microphone.

"Sure!" yelled Dandy. "Who would ever think of looking at the baggage of a bride and groom?"

"Shut up, Dandy!" I protested.

"Yah," yelled Dandy across at them. "Merry Christmas! Happy New Year! Wave the happy couple on their way, hey?"

The young constable got in the car with his com-

212

rade. Both bent to their radio, which began squawking stridently in response to the message they had sent.

It took about ten minutes.

Then the radio suddenly spat a brief message. The police car sprang into action. With a wild whoosh, it swung around, passing within a yard of ours. I had to jump.

"It's THEM!" shouted the blue-eyed constable. "They got 'em!"

And away in a cloud of dust.

"Dandy!" I cried, scrambling back behind my wheel, "We'll follow them! There'll be a reward! The Bankers' Association . . ."

"Hold it!" barked Dandy so loudly that Hortense woke up, even without her hearing aid.

"What is it?" she cried.

"Go back to sleep," said Dandy. "Let's drive on."

"But Dandy!" I protested. "You . . . you . . . it was you who . . . There's bound to be some kind of a reward from the Bankers' Association or somebody."

"Bankers!" said Dandy.

I looked at the old boy's irate grey eyes, dancing with fire.

I had forgotten that next to policemen, bankers are Dandy's pettest hate.

"Get cracking," he said, gesturing toward the bridge.

So we proceeded on through the pleasant countryside, the green fields waving in the breeze, the corn already man high, the boughs of the orchards beginning to bend.

"Cops!" Dandy kept muttering. "Plain as the nose on your face. Simplest gimmick since bank robbing was invented. Puh! I bet that kid will end up a sergeant!"

213

The Organization Man

WE WERE eighth in line in the queue at the hotel dining-room entrance when this gentleman came along.

He walked right past, up to head waiter guarding the door, menus in arm.

"Can you rig a table," said the gent, "for fourteen of us?"

"Not at the moment, sir," said the head waiter. "There is a line . . ."

"We're in 2501," said the important one. "Suite 2501, eh? Party of fourteen."

"It will be a good half-hour or more, sir."

"Make it sooner than that, will you?" suggested the gentleman. "Give me a ring when you've got it. Ask for Mr. Fimly."

He was not speaking quietly, as you or I would do under the circumstances. He was speaking with a tone of authority.

When he turned to leave, we in the queue could see he was one of those tall, fortyish, dashing types. Obviously an executive. Obviously fresh down from a cocktail party in Suite 2501. He had the exalted air of about the fifth Martini.

"Oh, by the way." He halted, calling back to the head waiter. "When you have the tables ready, I'll come down ahead and order the dinner."

"Very good, sir."

214

"Fimly," he said. "Mr. Fimly."

"Yes, sir."

Head waiters are hard to impress. This one was not impressed. He cast a calm, inscrutable eye over us in the queue.

In about ten minutes we came to the head of the queue and were graciously shown to a table for two, on the side, not too near the service doors.

We had finished our soup, which was essence of tomato, tingling, lean, golden red, and were well into our mixed grill, a chop, a kidney, a sausage, two rashers of bacon and a grilled half-tomato, with brittle hot shoestring potatoes (yum), when two waiters came along and started moving the tables next beside us, which had just been vacated.

They took three tables and set them in line together and began shaking out fresh tablecloths.

"Ah," said I. "The party from 2501."

I glanced at my watch: it was just the half-hour, as the head waiter had foretold.

In a moment, the head waiter arrived and, right behind him, the masterful gentleman we had already seen.

"Good," he said. "Put some flowers down the centre, eh?"

"Are there ladies in the party?" asked the head waiter.

"No, no," said the gentleman. "It's a party of businessmen. You'll doubtless recognize most of them."

"Yes, sir," said the head waiter, still unimpressed. "Did I understand you to say you would order the dinner?"

"Let me have the menu," said he. "And the wine list."

215

The head waiter handed over the menu and wine list.

"Set a place for me here," said the gentleman, "at the head of the table. I'll just glance over . . ."

And he sat down, while the waiters bustled about with silver and china, and the head waiter strolled off to his doorway.

We had a good chance now to size up the big shot. He was dressed smartly, one of those $150 hand-tailored dark greys. I bet he had been good-looking ten years ago. But he had that slightly worn look men get when they live too well. He was flushed. He was important. And he was excited to be important. Beautifully, oblivious of the fact that he was in a public dining-room full of his fellow men, he sat and studied the menu with alert attention.

Quietly, to Milne, my companion, I said:

"An organization man."

We slowed down on our mixed grills, because it would be interesting to see the party arrive.

In a few minutes, the head waiter returned.

"Have you decided, sir?"

"Not quite. But set up two wine glasses at each place. I want a red wine—Beaujolais, I think. Let me see what year you have."

And he picked up the wine list.

"I'll come back shortly, sir," said the head waiter. "Shall I telephone the room, sir?"

"No, no. They're on the way down."

The head waiter departed. Waiters arrived and set a collection of wine glasses at each place. The organization man had come to some decision. With a pencil, he made notations on both the menu and the wine list.

216

Then he sat back, satisfied, and turned to watch the entrance.

"Cocktail parties," I mentioned to Milne, "are hard to break up."

We couldn't stretch out our mixed grills any farther. Our waiter took our orders for dessert. Apple pie with Stilton for Milne. Oka cheese with wheaten biscuits for me. Coffee for Milne. Tea, with an extra pot of hot water, for me. I drink coffee only in Algiers, and then it is like syrup.

The head waiter, menus held high, approached.

"I will order now," announced the organization man.

"Mr. Fimly?" said the head waiter.

"That's correct."

"There's a message just come down for you, sir."

"Yes?"

"Your party has decided to go to a Chinese restaurant."

"They what?"

"They have left," said the head waiter, "for a Chinese restaurant."

"But good heavens! They were just coming down the . . ."

"Yes, sir," said the head waiter. "I just checked with the doorman. And your party left in taxis. They sent you the message."

The organization man rose angrily to his feet.

"WHICH Chinese restaurant?" he demanded thickly.

"They didn't say, sir."

With more hurry than becomes an organization man, Mr. Fimly wove his way among the tables, and he seemed to shrink as he went. Indeed, he was scuttling when he vanished through the entrance.

"Maybe," suggested Milne, "he is a bother to his friends."

"He likes to get things done," I supposed.

"He is the commanding type," reflected Milne.

The waiters came and rearranged the tables and took away the wine glasses. The head waiter had a look around, just in case the gentleman might have left a little paper of the realm.

We finished and went out and strolled around the lobby.

Mr. Fimly was standing humped over a telephone on the desk of the telephone enclosure.

He had the phone book open at the yellow pages.

Quite inexcusably, I went over and leaned on the counter too.

The yellow pages were open at Restaurants.

Mr. Fimly was calling the Chinese restaurants, one after the other.

The Pension

I ADMIT I wasn't quite as nimble as usual.

Just as I stepped off the curb, at the main downtown intersection, the yellow light flashed on. There were lots of pedestrians both coming and going in mid-section. So I kept on going.

But the red light caught me half-way, and I had to jump.

My old friend, the newsvendor on the northeast corner, with his arms full of papers, looked at me reproachfully as I scrambled on to the sidewalk.

"You don't want to try that stuff," he said, "at your age."

"Well, now," I replied heartily, glad of a pause to catch my wind, "just how old do you think I am, mister?"

"What I mean," said the newsie, "is that it doesn't do for elderly men to go galloping across intersections like that."

"I did all right," I pointed out, a little puffy. "But just how old do you think I am, eh?"

"O.K., how old ARE you?" countered the newsie, defensively.

"Well, sir," I said, "I'm not quite seventy. I'm to put in for my old-age pension any time."

"Aw, get away!" protested the newsie. "You're older than THAT!"

I looked at him in astonishment. Everybody tells me I look under sixty. I'm in the pink, they tell me. "How well you look," they say.

"No," I said firmly. "I have not put in for my pension YET."

"Well, well," said the newsie, and turned to hand papers to a couple of impatient passers-by.

I went on up the street in a preoccupied mood. I even forgot to look in the shop windows, and that is something. I was busy breathing good and deep, squaring my shoulders, and setting my hat at a little jauntier angle.

I watched the passing public, to see if any of them noticed me, how chipper I looked. But nobody did.

At the next intersection, who did I run into but Lawrie Till, the insurance man. He is very tall. I have to lean back to talk to him. But he saw me.

"Hello!" I said. "What's the matter with YOU?" Lawrie was looking tired out.

"I'm pooped," he said. "I'm just cleaning up everything at the office, and then my wife and I are going for a trip. Three weeks. Away from it all."

"Lawrie," I said, benevolently, "you do look as if you needed a rest."

He stretched up taller than ever and looked intently down at me.

"And what," he asked, "is the matter with YOU?"

"Eh?" I retorted, taking a youthful stance.

"How old are you now, Greg?" Lawrie asked.

"Aw, Lawrie," I laughed, "you ought to be good at guessing people's ages."

"Seventy-five?" hazarded Lawrie, doubtfully.

"I," I announced, for Lawrie's benefit, and that of anybody else in the passing crowd, "have NOT put in for my old-age pension yet."

"Nooooo!" said Lawrie.

We waved good-bye and were mutually swallowed up in the throng.

There is a post office on the main floor of the big department store. Miss Jenkins is there. She has been selling me stamps for . . . some time. I headed there.

"Miss Jenkins," I said, quietly, when my turn came, "have you got those forms for applying for your old-age pension?"

"Why, yes, Mr. Clark," said Miss Jenkins. "Haven't you put yours in YET?"

"Well, to tell the truth," I submitted, "my birthday is next Tuesday, when I come of age."

"Dear, dear!" said Miss Jenkins. "You are supposed to put them in six months ahead."

"Actually," I explained, "I have been kind of putting it off. I figure the government is sort of hard pressed, these last few months, and . . . uh . . ."

Miss Jenkins shook her head at me, and produced one of the yellow application forms. Discreetly she folded it and put it in one of those free brown envelopes they have in post offices, so that the people in the line-up behind me wouldn't notice.

I have always liked Miss Jenkins.

The bus bore me home, and I took off my coat and sat down and studied the yellow form.

I had just got to the place where they say that if you can't sign your name, an X will do, provided two people witness your X, when I heard boys' voices in my back yard. It is true nothing but zinnias remain in the garden. But I always react to boys' voices in the back yard.

It was young McPhedran and a boy I didn't know. About ten.

They had a catapult, and were crouched in the shrubbery, staring up at Prof. McNaught's house, next door.

I went out the back porch door.

"Boys," I said, "what are you up to?"

Young McPhedran is a very manly lad.

"Pigeons," said he. "We're shooting the pigeons."

As a director of the Canadian Audubon Society, I have my duty to perform.

"Look here, boys, I said, "you shouldn't shoot pigeons, or any other feathered creature."

"My dad," said young McPhedran, "says to chase them away. They are ruining the neighbourhood."

"Chase them, yes," I reasoned. "But don't SHOOT them."

"My dad says they hoot and holler in his window," said young McPhedran, "at five o'clock in the morning."

"Pigeons," I corrected, "coo."

"Not THESE pigeons," said young McPhedran, indicating the four or five fatties perched proprietorially on Prof. McNaught's roof.

"Look here, boys," I said, coming down off the porch. "What you want to do is scare the pigeons. Don't hit them. Shoot near them, and frighten them. Here, I'll show you."

I reached for the catapult, and young McPhedran surrendered it not too willingly. There was a stone about the size of a nutmeg in its leather.

"What you do," I explained, "is hit an eavestrough. The sound of the clank of the stone hitting the eaves-trough will send the pigeons flying for blocks. After a few scares, they won't come back."

I looked up at Prof. NcNaught's third storey. I selected my eavestrough. I took practised aim. After all, I owned a catapult . . . uh . . . some time ago.

"Now watch!" I directed.

Fffpoing!

The catapult was a dandy.

The stone hit the eavestrough, ricocheted off and went, clink, CRASH, tinkle-tinkle-tinkle, in Prof. McNaught's large attic window.

The boys ran one way. I ducked the other.

Breathing heavily, I sat down and filled out my old-age pension application.

And I would like to make you a small bet that I am the only Canadian out of more than eighteen million who has filled out his old-age pension application form ten minutes after breaking a professor's window with a catapult.

The Check-Out

IT is sometimes harder to check out of a hotel than
to check in, especially when they are all full up with
conventions.

The lobby was crowded when I came down from my
room at 3:15 P.M. That left me three-quarters of an
hour to check out and catch the four p.m. train home.

If there's anything I hate, it's a dither. I always allow
myself loads of time.

When I worked through the crowd in the lobby to
the cashier's wicket, I found seven people ahead of me.
Some people take an awful time paying a hotel bill.
They are probably the kind of people who travel on
credit cards, or who pay by cheque. And that always
means a lot of fiddle-diddling around while the cashier
checks with the credit manager, or examines identifica-
tions that these people have to dig out of their hip
pockets.

Cash. That's the way to pay a hotel bill.

I had kept a $20 bill out of my wallet, along with
my railway tickets, when I packed my wallet in with my
bush clothes. Twenty dollars would be ample. My room
for overnight would be around $12, and that would
leave me $8 for the taxi to the station here, the taxi
home, and a snack on the diner. And tips. With some
to spare.

To avoid all dither, I had taken my valise and duffle bag by taxi over to the station shortly after noon, and checked them through to Toronto.

By the time I was fourth in line at the cashier's wicket, it was 3:25. I could now see the cashier.

She was a young and suspicious woman. With cold dark eyes she studied each of my predecessors. She carried through the transactions of making change without a word. She never smiled. A difficult type of young woman.

It was 3:32 P.M. when I arrived at her wicket.

"Clark," I said. "Room 1882."

I laid my $20 bill down and slid it half under the metal grille that protected her from the public.

She turned her back to pick my card from the filing box behind her.

Somebody, somewhere, opened a door. A light draft blew my $20 bill. It started to slide in.

I shot my hand in under the low grille and made a slap at it.

Too late. It vanished over her cash drawer.

And at the slap, the cashier turned quickly and found me with my hand under her grille and within five inches of her cash drawer.

"My $20 bill!" I explained affably, withdrawing my hand. "A little gust of wind blew it in there . . ."

With my card in hand, she stepped back and surveyed the floor at her feet.

"I don't see it," she said.

"But my dear young lady," I protested. "It blew right in. It slid over that drawer there."

She disappeared from sight as she bent down, and when she came up, she just shook her head.

"Not here," she said. "Twelve-fifty. Any phone calls in the last few minutes?"

"But look," I quavered. "That $20 was all I had. It was all I took out of my wallet before I checked it with my bush clothes over at the station."

The man behind me gave an impatient cough. I glanced behind. There were eight in the queue.

"Can you pay by cheque?" asked the young lady.

"Of course, but . . ."

"Please see the credit manager, in the office to the left."

The clock showed 3:36 P.M.

"Armmffff!" said the man behind me.

So I broke out of the line and dodged the crowd to the credit manager's office.

He was busy when I opened his door. The person he was talking to was sitting down, relaxed.

"I . . . er . . . um . . ." I ventured.

"I'll see you in a moment," said he.

I closed the door and stood right outside it.

There were now nine people in the line-up at the cashier's wicket.

It was 3:41 P.M. when the door opened, and the man who came out took forty seconds to say good-bye to the credit manager.

"Briefly," I said, "I laid the only money I had on the counter of the cashier's desk. I am trying to catch the 4 P.M. train. A little gust of wind blew the bill in. I took my luggage over to the . . ."

"Wait a minute, wait a minute!" said the credit manager, soothing. "Now let's start all over again. What do you want me to do?"

"A cheque," I said. "Lend me a blank cheque. My

226

cheque book is in my wallet. I took it over right after lunch."

"Hold on!" said the credit manager. "Don't get excited. Have you any identification?"

"They're all in my wallet!" I cried.

"Can anybody identify you? Do you know anybody in town?"

"Mrs. Crawford!" I cried. "Mrs. Crawford, a great friend of my wife . . ."

"What's her number?"

It took us fifty-eight seconds to look her up in the book.

"I'll speak to her," said the credit manager, "and then hand you the phone."

He dialled. We waited.

"There is no answer," said the credit manager.

It was 3:46 P.M.

"What do I do?" I inquired.

"You should never leave things," said the credit manager, "to the last minute."

The door opened. The cashier appeared.

"Oh," she said, "you're the gentleman who lost the $20 bill." She held it in her hand.

With a cry, I staggered to my feet.

"It was on the floor," she explained.

"I know, I know!" I wailed.

She had brought me my bill and the change.

The credit manager and I shook hands in a sort of slither and I went out the door like a bat out of a barn. There was a taxi right at the door.

Into it like a groundhog into his hole. Full belt to the station, only five minutes.

No traffic. Everything wonderful.

Paid him twice what it was worth. Leaped out. Raced to the gate.

"Take it easy," said the gateman.

"Take it EASY?" I shouted.

The train was already drawing out. I raced after it. Its speed increased. I lost it.

Shrunken, I went back to the gateman.

"When" I asked bitterly, "is the next train for Toronto?"

"In five minutes," said the gateman. "Over on Track 4, there. That one you were chasing they're just moving out to the yards."

"Thank you," I said deeply.

"Never," said the gateman, "get in a dither."

Slowly, imperturbably, like a mud turtle, I toddled over to Track No. 4.